Broadway Christian Church Fort
The Dancer One Woman's Journey ...
Lee, Susan

P9-DNM-318

0000 0517

The Dancer

The Dancer

One Woman's Journey from Tragedy to Triumph

Susan Lee

PROPERTY OF
BROADWAY CHRISTIAN CHURCH LIBRARY
910 BROADWAY
FORT WAYNE, IN 46802

Foreword by
Don Smarto

BAKER BOOK HOUSE
Grand Rapids, Michigan 49516

Copyright 1991 by
Susan Lee

ISBN: 0-8010-5671-3

Printed in the United States of America

The prison profiles mentioned in this book do not reflect any one person. Rather, they are a combination of characters.

Scripture quotations used are from the New International Version © 1978 by New York International Bible Society. Those identified LB are from the Living Bible (Paraphrased) © 1971 Tyndale House Publishers, Wheaton, IL 60187.

Contents

I want to thank you,

Marv Wilson
for your guidance
encouragement
patience
wisdom

Nancy Friedenthal
my dearest friend
the first one I trusted
with "my words"

Mary Hendersen
for your enthusiastic support
of the Joy Dancers
and your treasured friendship

To

The Joy Dancers
those who were
those who are
those who will be.

*Dance
in his name
and the world
will look on
in wonder!*

Foreword

I was captivated by *The Dancer.* Susan Lee has expressed herself with compelling honesty in a story that is gripping, sensitive, and illuminating. This is a powerful book.

The Dancer is the kind of book that fills a special need; a need for victims to know there is a source of restoration. It is also important because of the growing crime rate in America. The Bureau of Justice Statistics, a division of the United States Department of Justice, indicates that rape is the fastest-growing violent crime in America.

Susan Lee's account of her brutal attack and her painful recovery is sad; it is also hopeful. This is because of the ultimate victory she realized when God used her brokenness to lead her to a deeper relationship with Christ and ultimately a unique ministry with prisoners.

Some of the things that happened to Susan could have destroyed some people. Victims of crimes such as rape are often crippled both mentally and physically. Yet Susan's story illustrates how God can use the bad things in life for his personal plans. As Paul clearly says in Romans 8:28, God may use suffering and tragic events for our individual, ultimate good.

The theme of forgiveness is clearly seen in Susan's story, too. I am confident that the greatest challenge Jesus called us to is the forgiveness of formidable enemies. Susan was the victim of a brutal felon and a violent crime. Perhaps this was the ultimate test of her faith. Rape is always a sick, stark, and ugly reality with sin at its very core. And there are no simple solutions for eradicating such violent crime. It is clear that institutions do not change people. Susan understands this. Also laws do not heal or comfort victims. She also knows this as a painful reality.

I like the balance in *The Dancer.* It is important to have compassion for victims and to staunchly uphold their rights while, simultaneously, hoping for restoration and healing in the lives of offenders. I appreciate Susan's honesty about her anger. God understands our emotions, and Susan gives the reader—who may be a potential victim—permission to work through very understandable human emotions.

I am delighted to learn about Susan's dance ministry in women's prisons. With all the attention male prisoners receive in the media, the special needs of incarcerated women are often ignored.

Susan Lee by her life demonstrates a transformation from a basically self-centered individual to someone with a true servant's heart. She has overcome adversity with courage and hope. What also comes out clearly in *The Dancer* is the need to move away from preoccupation with self and the gratification of ego to prepare for sacrifice as a servant. Christ said we will find our life when we lose it. Out of the brokenness of Susan's suffering has come the triumph of a life directed by compassion toward other suffering people.

DON SMARTO
Director, Institute for Prison Ministries
Billy Graham Center

... love rarely ever reaches out to save
except it does it with a broken hand.

—Calvin Miller in *The Singer*

Dancing in the Dark

1 December 1981, 5:50 P.M.

I sprint in and lunge for the locker room, briefcase in one hand, dance bag in the other. In rhythmic, almost choreographed movements, I peel off a well-tailored three-piece suit, unraveling the pinstriped perfection of my corporate persona. Sliding the pink leg warmers over the well-worn aerobic shoes, my thoughts flash back to the office.

Overall, it was a good day. My presentation was a big hit. Now all the top brass know my name. That ought to count for something. And, as usual, I did it all myself. Ann, that incompetent assistant of mine, messed up all my overheads. What a dope! I yelled at her, and then Karen got upset because she wants our department to be all sweetness and light. Karen claims to be a Christian. I say she's a religious fanatic. But that's her trip, not mine. Anyway, I'm better at work than church stuff. That's what I told Karen: I believe in the concept of God, but anything more is just intellectual suicide. It hinders the creative process. It destroys the individual. It breeds followers, not leaders. Count me out! I was meant for center stage. No doubt about that! Shoot!—it's almost six. I'll lose my spot in front of the mirror!

6:00 P.M.

"Hold! two, three, four . . . don't you dare waver! . . . five, six, seven . . . release! Okay, take it up slowly . . . now higher . . . let's go for the burn!"

Drat! I've pulled something. But I'm not going to stop. I'm going to tough it out and keep dancing. I'll grab the teacher after class. Maybe she'll have a miracle cure. No pain, no gain! That's what they say!

7:00 P.M.

Whew! What a workout! I've got to get to the teacher before everyone crowds around her. Oh, too late. Why don't these foolish people get out of the way. I need to speak with her now. This stinks! I'm second to last in line. There's another injured dancer in back of me. What a waste of my time. The whole class has gone except for us.

"Scuse us, any of youse three ladies know where we can find a maintenance man around here? No? No guy around here? Well, that's all right. Thanks anyhow."

"As your teacher I'm advising that we walk each other to our cars. I don't know what those two are doing here. They give me the creeps. We can just . . ."

"Okay, down on the floor or we'll blow your heads off! These guns are real. Don't make us use them. Give us your purses.

"You, blondie, get over there and take off your clothes!"

Oh, my God, he's talking to me! I'm going to be raped. Please God, help. If you loved me you wouldn't let this happen to me. I don't deserve this. God, where are you?

"Hurry up, or I'll knock all your teeth out!"

God, he keeps hitting me, and I can't get my shoes off. Oh, Lord, he smells awful . . . like liquor . . . like grease . . . like dirt . . . I'm gagging. . . .

I'm hurting. . . . I'm bleeding. . . . My teeth are loose. . . . And he's raping me. . . . I'm going to die. . . . I want to die. . . . I can't stand it. . . . Let him shoot me, and it will be over. . . . Please, God. . . .

He's stopping. . . . It's over. . . . He's cutting the wires from the teacher's recorder . . .

"Turn over. I mean it now; I'll use this thing. Lie face down. Put your hands behind your back. . . ."

Then silence, punctuated by staccato breathing and muffled sobs.

God, where are you—are you there? God, if you let me live through this, I will try to find you again. I did love you once, as a child, but somewhere along the way I got too busy, too smart, too self-reliant. I thought I didn't need you. I thought I knew it all. But I need you now! Imagine me, with all my degrees and my successful career, tied up here like a dog. But you were tied up, too, weren't you—nailed, even. They beat you up, too, and you were innocent.

Lord, if I survive, I'll try to find you—to find what you want from me. I'll put you first. I'll use my talents for your honor.

If you let me live, I'll live for you. . . .

9:00 P.M.

"Police. Everybody stay where you are. You first, lady. Give me your hands and I'll untie you. . . . What on earth happened here?"

"We were robbed and that blonde girl over there was raped. I'm her dance teacher. I need to go to her."

"Wait. Let us handle her. You shouldn't touch her because she needs to be examined for fingerprints. She can't wash. Her clothes need to be checked, too. She's bleeding. She needs a doctor.

"Are you okay, Miss?"

Stunned, shivering, blood oozing from my mouth, I snatch my broken teeth from the floor with lacerated hands and think, *I'll never be the same again.*

And I never was.

What followed was an eight-year odyssey—a spiritual, physical, and mental journey that took me places I had never intended to go. That night of terror cut me off from my previous life as surely as a knife severs a rope.

Gone forever was that golden dancer—so confident, so fearless, so sure of my ability to do whatever I wanted. Although my pain and confusion clouded my perception, deep within my soul a new dance was beginning. I was no longer dancing solo.

Prima in Pieces

10:00 P.M., Hospital

"Seventeen years as a cop and I've never seen any-thing like it. They were all in a semicircle—face down, hands tied behind their backs, blood everywhere. She was in the middle, quivering, her whole body a whimper. You know, she looks like the girl next door. I see her and I see my daughter, my sister, my wife. I feel for her. But then I file the report and she just becomes another statis-tic. What can I do?

"I told her we'll catch those stinkers no matter what it takes. I promised her we'd send a detective out right away . . . I gave my word. I wonder if she'll get over this completely. I mean, it has to change a person. How many recover? Are they ever really normal again?"

He has such a loud voice. Doesn't he know I can hear every-thing he says? His face is crimson, and he's so big. Every time he questions me about it, he breaks out in a sweat. He's so over-

*weight I'm afraid he will have a heart attack. Ironic—that I'm
worried about him. But I'm not likely to have one—the benefit
of dance and aerobics: an athlete's heart.*

*The ambulance ride was short . . . like I dreamed it. One
green pill, one orange, and one shot in the arm—that's what the
nurse gave me. She said for someone my size it should calm me
down—knock me out, even—but I still can't stop shaking. . . .
She said the doctor would be along shortly, then she left me alone
with this cop.*

*He chooses his words carefully. He is trying to be gentle, sen-
sitive. He looks at me intently, like he is watching a drama and
waiting for the climax.*

*So this is what it feels like to be a rape victim. This is how
people react to you . . . how they look at you . . . how they treat
you. Like a fragile prima ballerina . . . a prima in pieces.*

*"The hour I first believed. . . ." Lines from the hymn
"Amazing Grace" keep floating through my head; it's one of the
few religious songs I know. "Amazing grace! how sweet the
sound—That saved a wretch like me! I once was lost but now
am found, Was blind but now I see." I read somewhere that it
was Elvis Presley's favorite.*

*Elvis . . . hymns . . . the plump cop. . . . Maybe I've gone
insane—or maybe I just can't stand to think about what's happened.*

*Where is the doctor? They make you wait so long. Questions . . .
questions . . . they ask a million questions. Insurance? Am I pregnant? Am I on drugs? Me? I'm not the criminal. . . .*

*God, I need you. Please let me feel your presence. I'm alive!
I survived! But I'm broken in a million pieces. Remember the
promise I made to you on that floor? I meant it. But I'm scared.
I don't know what to do. I'm alone here on the West Coast; I
only know a few people from work. It's just you and me, Jesus.
Help me. . . .*

"You're pretty badly beaten, but no broken bones . . .
no broken cheekbones. The bruises and cuts will heal;
you'll just need to have most of your teeth replaced;

you'll want to see a dentist soon. I'll give you a prescription to prevent infection. That's it. You can go home now."

"But Doctor, I'm afraid to drive home. I'm not from around here. I'm from Boston. I have no license, no money, no purse. They stole everything. Can't I stay overnight? Then I can call someone from work in the morning. . . ."

"Call someone now."

"Alright . . . I will, but . . ."

"Sorry, Miss. We have no available beds. The nurse will clean you up, and then take you to the phone. You can stay here until someone comes for you. But then you have to go."

With that abrupt adieu came the challenge of facing the rest of my life as a member of an exclusive club. The dues are high and the initiation painful, but the membership is for life. The roster includes groups of people admitted solely because of nationality; others got in because of religious beliefs, while others make it because of skin color. Some are just in the wrong place at the wrong time and become pawns in the politics of terrorism. Some are newborns christened with the surname "crack baby." Individuals too can become members. One woman was merely a lone jogger in Central Park!

The price of admission to this club? You must be a victim.

Victim. Webster defines it as any sufferer from a destructive, injurious, or adverse action or agency—a person or animal sacrificed or regarded as a sacrifice. The term can apply to an individual or it can encompass an entire group, as with the Holocaust.

Rape victims make up a very exclusive club. One out of three women will be raped sometime during her life.

And of those women, the prognosis for recovery is not always positive. Some women have committed suicide as late as two years after a rape experience.

I was to find out later that the doctor's curt response to me was indicative of the world's response to victims. A lot of people don't want us around because we remind them that bad things can happen to innocent people in ordinary circumstances.

What could be more ordinary than an aerobic dance class at six in the evening? I wasn't at fault. I couldn't have done anything to prevent it. And that is what scares them—happenstance, a flash of fate, the frightening possibility that a person's life can change in an instant. No one wants to believe rape can happen to them, and the sight of a rape victim reminds them that it can. And so too often, they try to avoid you.

True to their word, the day after the rape the Los Angeles Police Department phoned to confirm that the department had assigned a detective to my case. He would stop by to see me.

Victimization is not limited to those who have been on the receiving end of crime. In today's violent times, many police officers are victims of stress-related illnesses. My detective had an ulcer. He had just finished an investigation of child abuse when he was assigned to my case. He had promised himself for the sake of his ulcer that he would never again get personally involved in a case.

However, as he explained it, "I figured this would be easy. Some stuck-up broad from Boston. But then I opened the door and there you were, all red-eyed and shaking. And I thought, there goes my ulcer."

The Lord was watching out for me with this kind and decent detective. But he also introduced me to a side of police work that gave me nightmares—line-ups!

Line-ups are nothing like you see on television, where one person views a line of alleged criminals. Instead, victims are shuffled from one room to another. Then, huddled together in an overcrowded room, they watch as criminals, behind glass, are marched out on stage like movie stars.

I'd like to turn back the pages of a journal I kept in the months after my rape. This was my first impression of fellow victims:

> Beaten, dazed, exhausted, silent people with stone faces, symbols of muted agony . . . eyes darting . . . suspicious of everyone. . . . Some clutched purses to their chests as if protecting an infant. One man repeatedly removed his wallet and counted the contents. An older woman nervously removed the spotless white gloves from her hands to reveal a missing finger on her left hand. During a robbery she was told to take the ring off. Years of marriage and a few extra pounds had rendered the ring stuck for life. To get it, the robber cut her finger off.

And then there were the survivors' tales:

> Monday night football on a balmy California night, front door open to let in the breeze. . . . Father and son watching the game. Mom and two neighborhood women styling each other's hair. Suddenly six men with sawed-off shotguns walk right through the front door. They tie up father and son. Then each of the six men rapes each of the women. Father and son look on helplessly.

The epitome of man's inhumanity to man:

> At a Los Angeles street corner, a woman gets out of her car to call home to check on her infant son. Five men grab her, rape her, torture her, then take her keys and run over her with her own car.

That woman survived. Many don't. So those of us who do feel compelled to tell the tale for them—for those who didn't make it. We feel the responsibility of memory.

The maimed. The tortured. The crime victims. They are the modern-day victims—pawns in the hands of criminals fulfilling themselves through cruelty. And I was one of the broken. I cried at every line-up.

My detective once cautioned me, "If you see the rapist, don't show any emotion, or they will say you are prejudicing the others."

I answered, "I don't see him. It's just that everyone up there is so ugly, it scares me."

He responded, "Well, I'll try to have them arrested for showing an obscene face in public."

Humor in the face of adversity. My detective tried that and everything he could think of to make the weekly line-up experience a little less frightening. It didn't work.

I developed a constant tremor in my right hand. In front of other people, I would only drink coffee from a Styrofoam® cup because the rattling of china attracted so much attention. Sleeping and eating were impossible. Someone referred me to a psychiatrist, and I began the painful journey of trying to understand what had happened to me.

I also began, blindly and hesitantly, to reach toward God. Something really had happened to me spiritually that night as I lay bound and bleeding on the dance floor. I had made a very real commitment to the Lord and had asked him to come into my heart. Deep inside, I knew that commitment would change my life. But I was still too shocked and broken to trust God totally through the recovery process.

I was like a frightened animal lost in the woods, not knowing which way to turn. I was too terrified to put out my trash, let alone look for a church. So a friend suggested a television broadcast, the *In Touch* program with Dr. Charles Stanley. The first night I tuned in, he was beginning a series titled "Advancing through Adversity." He told the story of Saul of Tarsus, who became the apostle Paul.

Saul of Tarsus, the Bible says, was strong, fierce, and intellectual, intense in his desire to rid the world of the Christian faith. He used torture to try to make Christians curse Christ. Saul stood by and held the coats of his fellow persecutors as they stoned the Christian deacon Stephen. He listened as the dying Stephen prayed for his murderers. But even this didn't faze Saul. He had heard about the miracles of Jesus Christ—the way he had raised people from the dead and miraculously healed people, the tremendous truths that he spoke. But Saul was still determined to rid the earth of all Christians.

Cocky, proud, egotistical, single-minded—Saul was commissioned by the Jewish high priests to track down Christians in foreign lands. And so he set off with his companions on the road to Damascus. Saul recounts what happened next:

> I was on such a mission to Damascus, armed with the authority of the high priests, when one day about noon, a light from heaven brighter than the sun shone down on me and my companions. We all fell down, and I heard a voice speaking to me, "Saul, Saul why are you persecuting me? You are only hurting yourself."
>
> "Who are you, sir?" I asked.
>
> "I am Jesus, the one you are persecuting. Now stand up! For I have appeared to you to appoint you as my servant and my witness. You are to tell the world about this experience—to open their eyes so that they may turn from darkness to light." (Acts 26:12–16 LB)

Struck blind by this event on the Damascus road, Saul was born into the kingdom of God amid adversity. Scared,

PROPERTY OF
BROADWAY CHRISTIAN CHURCH LIBRARY
910 BROADWAY
FORT WAYNE, IN 46802

humiliated, his entire career wiped out, Saul thought he was blind for life. Saved in the midst of other persecutors, Saul joined the Christians he had intended to kill.

Conversion of a soul is the miracle of a moment. The making of a saint is the task of a lifetime. When Saul, renamed Paul, got up off that Damascus road, he had been changed, but it took him fourteen years to begin his preaching. But what seemed to be the absolute end to his career was the beginning of a far greater one. Paul became one of God's greatest men, second only to Jesus in his impact.

I listened. I wept. I believed. I identified with Saul's experience. But I still had a long recovery ahead. I lived in constant fear. I was afraid of strangers, afraid of the dark, and—most of all—afraid that it might happen again.

Evidence of my smashed self is best related in this encounter with my psychiatrist:

"Can you promise me that I'll never be raped again?"

"No. No one could promise that."

"I thought that's what you'd say. So I'm preparing myself. Every night I go through this ritual. I go into my bathroom and I stand in front of the mirror and I stare. Then I flash back to the night of the rape . . . how scared I was . . . how much it hurt. But I know that next time it will be worse. So I force myself to picture the rapist pulling out a knife and slashing my face. I make myself feel the pain, the terror, the devastation of a ruined face. Because if I prepare myself—then, when it really happens—maybe it won't hurt so much. Maybe I won't be as scared as I was the first time . . . maybe . . . maybe. . . ."

Break Dance

Susan called me that night. I went to the hospital to pick her up. I saw the other two. No doubt in my mind why she was chosen. She was the prettiest one, and she has that gorgeous long hair. That's why they picked her to rape. I'm sure of it. . . . Come on—your makeup looks fine. Our break is over. I have to get back to my desk."

There I sat—long hair and all—behind the door of a stall in that ladies' room. I felt like a victim once again—a victim of bored fellow workers hungry for sensational bits to spice up an otherwise routine day. The voices of gossip spouted various opinions on what had brought about this calamity in my life. Today it was my hair.

I left the ladies' room, my neck tense with the daily effort of keeping my head high. Till five o'clock every day I tried to keep up the charade of a miraculous recovery—emotions intact. I worked hard to show I was ready to resume my life and pick up where I had left off, to act as if nothing had happened. To the world I appeared to be a "together" woman when in reality all that was left were shards of a smashed self.

Daily I trod a high, thin wire, mindful of the abyss below. It was an exhausting balancing act between sanity and insanity—between the real world and the subtext in my mind.

Voices ran constantly through my head, never giving me a moment's peace. There were many. The voices of the gossips. The police. Concerned friends. And his—the rapist's—the loudest voice that echoed incessantly, punctuating my every activity. While brushing my teeth, washing dishes, standing at the water cooler, driving my car, I heard it: *"You get over there and take off your clothes."* I couldn't get rid of that voice.

Driving home from work with clenched teeth, tightly gripping the steering wheel, emotions ready to spill, I barely made the ten-minute ride each night.

Finally, safe inside, my tiny apartment seemed to become the framework of a surrealistic painting, where phantasmagoric figures escaped from their frame into my living room. Nightly they gave an enervating performance that ranged from ranting and raving to weeping and whimpering.

My eight-hour office portrayal of tightly sealed emotions and total control, gave way to abandon—one final, primal scream that seemingly was my best defense against madness.

Totally spent, I crawled into bed to catch one or two hours of fitful rest, but not sleep—sleep meant uncontrollable nightmares.

Lying awake and staring at the ceiling dappled with the shadows of the street light, I heard strange, suspicious sounds and imagined prowlers. I compulsively checked and rechecked locked doors and windows once, twice, three times, till the chirping of birds and the light of early dawn heralded the haven of morning. Then, barely functioning, I again donned my corporate garb to re-create my role as "the businesswoman."

Before I left the house each day, I fanatically hid anything of value; I was convinced that I would be robbed again. Tearing off squares of aluminum foil, I wrapped up all my credit cards and put them in the refrigerator. *With my luck,* I thought cynically, *I'll get a hungry burglar who thinks the silver wrappings contain food.*

Driving home this particular Friday night, something else was bothering me.

She has that gorgeous long hair.

I couldn't get that phrase out of my mind. Was that why they picked me? Was I to blame? Did my hair attract attention? Never again did I want to be noticed. I just wanted to blend in with the crowd. I didn't want to be chosen.

Frantically, I opened the three locks on my front door. I knew what I had to do. I went straight to my sewing box and then hurried into the bathroom. With trembling but determined hands, I cut off the silky strands that had once been my pride and joy, that had saucily bounced to dance tunes, that had kept me warm during New England winters, that represented youth, vitality, and above all femininity. Soon my hair was almost all gone, and I didn't care. I didn't want to be pretty. I just wanted to be safe.

Breathless, perspiring, and slightly delirious, I looked from the hair-strewn floor to the mirror. I had scalped myself and left jagged, uneven wisps in place of golden locks. Coming to my senses, I vowed to visit a hairdresser the next day.

To many women, hairdressers are like bartenders—true confessors, psychiatrists, best friends, counselors. Realizing that my new hairdo was not the result of a talent for precision cutting, my stylist gently inquired. Needing someone to talk to, I told him the whole story.

He responded, "I'm a Christian, and I know God doesn't want you to make yourself unattractive. It is a myth that only attractive women are raped. It wasn't your fault what happened. We live in a fallen world, and bad things happen to good people. But you've come to the Lord now, and he will help. And because he is God, he can creatively take bad things and weave them into something beautiful. I know you can't believe that now, but in time you'll see."

Patched up, primped and polished with a shorter but professional-looking coif, I emerged from the salon an hour or two later. My hairdresser, sensitive to the fact that I was still apprehensive about walking alone even in early afternoon, graciously escorted me to my car. Then he did a remarkable thing; he got into my car and prayed with me. I wasn't used to this. In my mind, you only prayed in church or when you cried out to God in trouble. But my hairdresser said that coming to the Lord at any time was the privilege of knowing and accepting a personal God and that I, too, had this privilege.

It seemed now that everywhere I went I met Christians in all walks of life: doctors, the police artist, work colleagues, dancers. It was as if God was surrounding me with legions of his own to protect me. The family of God was everywhere.

Still, I was very anxious. I found it difficult, if not impossible, to swallow solid food, so I existed on liquids alone. My weight plummeted.

A kind woman from work offered me her home; she thought that living with a family might relieve my fear. She was recently divorced with two small children; I was awaiting a transfer back to Massachusetts. The situation would be temporary.

The same week that I moved in, this woman's house was robbed. When we found out, I became hysterical.

Wherever I went, criminals found me. I felt like a lone Jew among Nazis. It seemed that nowhere was safe. I trembled uncontrollably. My mind felt blurry, foggy. I could hear my heart thumping, and those incessant voices within. I felt like I was losing my mind.

I needed to talk to someone from home—someone who could reassure me that I could hold on.

In the aftermath of rape the hardest thing to deal with is friends and family who respond inadequately when the victim is in desperate need.

Let me re-create the scene the day of the robbery as I made that one phone call to save my sanity:

"Peggy's house has just been robbed and I need to talk with someone from home. I feel like I'm losing my mind."

"Well, what do you expect me to do three thousand miles away? Go find some doctor to give you a pill. I was taking a nap, and you woke me up. Now don't bother me with things I can't do anything about." Click!

Click went the phone—and snap went my mind. I felt something break loose inside. Then, in a jumble of actions and feelings, many things happened simultaneously. I heard or felt a buzzing, an inexplicable inner sensation. It was something like an electric shock, combined with a vibration—like a heavy metal spring being suddenly coiled and uncoiled. I felt like I was in another dimension, eerie, misty, foggy. And worse even than this haze was the sensation of losing all power, a terrifying seepage of strength and of sanity.

I had an appointment that day with my psychiatrist. Somehow, I made it to his office. I told of the day's events, from the robbery to the phone call to the feeling that my mind had snapped. He had spoken to me before about entering a hospital. I thought the purpose was to get my appetite and sleeping patterns back. Now he told me gently, "Susan, I really think that you need to be hospitalized—and not just for the physical reasons. You see, they are symptomatic of the turmoil your mind is in."

"Oh, my God. You're talking about a mental institution!"

"Well, yes—a hospital like that."

"I'm not crazy. I just had something terrible happen to me. Can't you understand that?"

"Yes, I can. And you're not crazy. You're suffering from something known as post-traumatic stress syndrome—a result of the trauma that you have gone through. It is a kind of delayed reaction to the rape. The mind, to protect itself, initially shuts down and denies the event. But your subconscious doesn't forget, and it eats away at you till you face it."

"But a hospital like that will just scare me."

"You have a stereotype in your mind. The hospital I'm thinking of is a beautiful place. There is only one caveat. Once you enter, it is on your record for life, and anyone who investigates your past can find it out. If you remain in a normal profession this shouldn't hurt you. If you chose a more visible career—say, something like politics—an issue could be made. But I think it's a risk worth taking."

"What if I refuse to go?"

"You can. You're the one who has to sign yourself in. But if you refuse, you may never recover, and then someone would have to commit you—maybe for life. You've had a partial breakdown. Don't wait till you've broken down completely."

My God, where are you? How can you let this happen to me? Haven't I suffered enough? The Bible says that you won't break a bruised reed. Yeah, well, I've snapped. How many more bruises can I take? You've taken away all my pride, and now my self-respect. Will I ever function normally again? Do you care, God?

The Dancer Returns

two days after my psychiatrist recommended a hospital stay, I drove myself to a secluded estate with lots of trees and flowers, a place very different from the clinical, antiseptic environment I expected. I was greeted at the door by a pleasant, matronly receptionist, who admitted me. She then reached under her desk and touched something. Two female attendants arrived and escorted me into a room.

This won't be so bad after all, I was thinking . . . and then it happened. They stood on either side of me. One took my coat and sweater; the other took my purse and emptied out the contents on a flat table. Quickly and nimbly she sifted through my things, while the other investigated the pocket of my coat and sweater. They looked surprised when I began to tremble again.

Don't they know that's what the rapist did to my purse and all my belongings? Don't they know it's like being raped again?

The spoils of their pillaging included a nail file, nail polish remover, glue, aspirin, barrettes, and rubber bands. These items they appropriated, trying to explain that other patients might try to harm themselves.

And then came the ultimate degradation. I had to remove my clothing in front of them to make sure I wasn't harboring any drugs or weapons of any kind. I hesitated, humiliated. Then, as I reached down to untie my shoes, I remembered a passage I had read that morning from *Each New Day,* a daily devotional written by Corrie ten Boom, the Dutch Christian who had been sent to a Nazi concentration camp for hiding Jews in her home during World War II. Corrie had written,

> In the concentration camp we went through the ordeal of being stripped of all our clothing and made to stand for several hours. It was more difficult than anything else we experienced. . . . As I stood there it was as if I saw Jesus at the cross. The Bible tells us they took away His garments and He hung there naked. Through my suffering, I understood a fraction of the suffering of Jesus.[1]

As I remembered those words, a strange peace enveloped me. I sensed the presence of God and seemed to feel his loving arms around me even during this embarrassing moment. A few days ago I had cried out, asking if God cared. He was giving me an answer. I was now stripped of everything—pride, possessions, identity, respect. To these hospital personnel I was just another troubled body—no one special. I had suffered rape and brokenness, and now was entering a mental institution. What could be worse? But this inexplicable peace told me I would somehow make it. I might falter. I might question God again. But somehow he would bring me through it all.

A routine physical followed the humiliating search. My vital signs were taken, and I was weighed and measured. I would find out later that I was to be weighed daily because weight fluctuations could signal depression and thus extend the hospital stay. That realization was shock treatment enough to bring back my appetite! Appropriately enough, the first place they took me was to the cafeteria for an early dinner.

In sharp contrast to my expectation of a drab mental hospital was a dining room replete with every bright shade on the color wheel. It was as if a psychiatrist-turned-artist had dipped his brush into a palette of optimism and in broad strokes painted the surroundings as he wished life to be. Such an artist could control the hue of the decor, but not the unmistakable doomsday aura of the patients.

Broken spirits with faces of despair and submission shuffled in to repeat the reluctant ritual of a hospital meal. Looking from one to the other, I wondered what had brought them here. Were they also victims of crime? Had they been abused? What cruel blow had life dealt them?

"She just had shock treatment," my dining mate volunteered, pointing to a corner table. "All of them over there have had the treatments."

I saw a mass of organisms with a human shape attired in cadaverous grey hospital garb, a symbol of their almost-extinguished humanity. They stood out from the rest of us, who were allowed to wear jeans. Something else was different too—their eyes seemed dead. I thought the whole table emitted a whiff of the grave.

My table was different. Energy abounded. Nervous tapping and clanking of silverware were the norm. Another new arrival and her boyfriend, who was staying through the meal, joined our group. He explained that she was a bulimic, and even though she seemed painfully thin and barely touched her food, he said she might come

down at night and devour the contents of the kitchen—
then go back to her room and "purge."

Another woman was pregnant for the fourth time. She
had previously lost all three babies for unknown reasons.
She seemed all right physically, so her doctor thought the
problem might be psychological. To safeguard this preg-
nancy, her family had hospitalized her.

I thought about all these people as I lay in bed that
night trying to sleep. What did they do to deserve this?
What did *I* do to deserve this? If God was everywhere,
was he in here, too? Or did he make it a habit to stay out
of mental institutions?

*Lord, do you hear me? What is the purpose of all this? Will it
make me a better person? Are you trying to teach me something—humility, sensitivity? In the troubled eyes of these
patients, can I still see you?*

I wasn't prepared for what would happen the next day.
It was a group therapy session, supposedly intended to
help people open up and see that they shared common
problems. But I don't think they were that meticulous in
placing people in groups. Or perhaps they had no other
patients in my situation. But they put me in a group of
women who had all attempted suicide.

Suicide. The word shocks, and it silences. And so it did
to this sullen group until one very large, very heavy black
woman hissed at me, "What are you in here for? What
could possibly be wrong with you, with your pretty little
face and your pretty little body?"

I froze. I couldn't move. I couldn't speak. I was terrified. Everyone, including the counselor, seemed to be
waiting for my response.

All my life I've been "mouthy." Words were my business. I used them to persuade, to cajole—mainly to get
whatever I wanted. I used my communication skills to

get out of traffic violations, to get jobs, raises, bargains. I always stood up for my rights. No one pushed me around.

But look at me now. I cowered before this woman. I shook visibly. I just wanted to get out of there. The counselor moved on to other people, but this woman glowered at me the entire hour as if I represented something she hated.

My next appointment was alone with my psychiatrist. When I related this harrowing encounter, he explained that her reason for attacking me was probably much the same as the rapist's. In my appearance and my demeanor, I represented the establishment She probably felt that her economic plight and less-than-adequate lifestyle was due to an unfair society—which, to her, I symbolized.

For me, this hospitalization was my humbling. I had always prided myself on intellectual achievements and talents. I was a straight-A student, a magna cum laude graduate. And I really thought that I was better than most people, especially the kind of people hospitalized here. I figured their problems were due to weakness—their lack of employment to laziness; their emotional breakdowns to genetic, inherited deficiencies.

And now I was one of them—a patient in an institution that questioned my sanity. My pride, which had propelled me to achieve and excel, was smashed. My arrogance was totally gone.

Never again would I think I was superior to others. Never again could I hear the cackling of pan handlers or see the incessant twitching of a bag lady, the trembling hands of an alcoholic, the begging of street children, the writhing of the addicted, the frozen resignation of the homeless without feeling compassion. Never again could I see and hear these things and look down my arrogant nose. Because, you see, I was one of them. Even today, whenever I feel a little too self-important, the Lord reminds me of this hospital stay.

My psychiatrist concluded our visit with a statement for me to think about: "The makers of oriental rugs deliberately weave a single flaw into their complex patterns because perfection is a divine, not a human, prerogative. Welcome to the world of the flawed, Susan!"

It was true. I had been driven to perfection in every area of my life. I was the quintessential member of the "me" generation lost in visions of perfection, of being forever healthy, young, beautiful, and strong. And in this fanatical pursuit, I never saw the need for compassion and sensitivity. Those virtues just got in my way.

There is nothing wrong with a healthy self-esteem and taking care of oneself in a difficult world. But I had been self-absorbed, catering to *only* myself. Now I began to realize that it is important to stop, to smell the roses, and to reach out to others less fortunate than I.

That night I was able to think of my therapy group as human beings—not disturbed, violent animals driven to suicide to put themselves out of their own misery. Something had driven them to this point, suggested my new, compassionate nature. And there but for the grace of God went I. I still didn't know how to handle that one angry woman in my group, but I drifted off to sleep before I could figure it out.

Bracing myself for another tense day, I entered the group-therapy room, taking a seat beside the counselor for protection. It was one minute to nine, and she hadn't appeared yet. Maybe I was safe. Then she waddled through the back door and plopped right down beside me. Before the counselor could begin, she put her face close to mine and snarled, "I wanna know what you're doin' here. What are you in here for?"

"I was raped. That's right, raped. You tried to take your life. I fought for mine. I looked death in the face and I survived. And you know, I'm going to make it. Because

I'm not blaming society for what happened to me. I'm just looking to God and trying to go on with my life. And if you're smart, you will too."

I sat down shaking, shadowing my eyes with my hands, head bowed. I hadn't planned to jump up and counter her with my story. It was as if a force had come over me—an old force that I hadn't had for months now. I felt stronger.

And then a strange thing happened. I looked up, and in front of me was a big, awkward but outstretched hand. I looked into her face, which had softened, and I saw that her eyes were filled with tears.

"I had no idea," she said.

I smiled slightly, and tentatively took her hand. "It's okay," I offered.

When I left that room, I had taken another step toward recovery. My terror had subsided. The tremor in my right hand was lessening, and for the first time in months, I was hungry.

As the days passed, I got bolder, feistier, and a little more outspoken. My therapy group began to look to me as a leader—someone with guts.

As I got better, I started to pay more attention to my surroundings. And I noticed that almost everyone in the hospital sat around and watched television all day. No one exercised or even walked much. Then they would complain that they were getting fatter, and this would make them more depressed.

One day, I was sitting in the large room where we all assembled. As usual, the TV was blaring, and everyone was staring like zombies at the screen. And suddenly I heard myself say:

"You people have to get moving."

I jumped up, turned off the TV, and flipped on the radio. Before anyone could object, I started dancing in the middle of the room. The song, from the new movie

Flashdance, was titled "Maniac," ironic considering our place of containment.

They formed a circle around me and started clapping, urging me to keep it up. I looked around at the faces.

I had lived in that place for a week now with these people. We shared a special bond, a bond that unites victims and fellow sufferers—a bond of collective terror, collective anxiety, collective anguish.

"Let's see you do thirty jumping jacks. Look, she's doing it. Way to go!"

"Join in," I challenged.

To my surprise, several did. Clapping, singing, and laughing surrounded us.

"Susan, your doctor—he wants to speak with you."

I stopped abruptly and turned around. There was my psychiatrist standing in the hallway, watching my whole routine. I hurried toward him, not knowing what to expect.

"I don't need the roof to fall in on me. I know you are stronger, and pretty much back to your old self. You can go home now."

Never was I so happy to obey a doctor's order. I made arrangements for my departure and packed quickly. I said good-bye to my fellow patients and told them to keep praying and keep dancing. But I felt a strange sense of sadness and foreboding, not knowing if they would all make it.

It has been said that compassion is feeling your pain in my heart. I had developed compassion in this hospital.

I walked out that door, never looking back. Behind me I heard the doors lock, blocking out the bustling noise of hospital activity. I stepped out into the noonday sun and felt its penetrating rays on my pallid face. I was free.

My hands were steady. My walk was brisk. And I vowed, as God was my judge, that I would never be a victim again.

The Dance of Anger

everybody on the dance floor. Let's work, class. Hear that music? Now let the rhythm take control. Pump it up!"

It was my fifth aerobics class that day, and I still felt tense, tight, angry. I knew that the only way I could sleep that night was to take one more class. But my legs were aching, my back was sore, and my feet were ready to fall off. No way could I "pump it up" as the instructor suggested. But I kept going. *Just one more class.*

I felt tiny beads of sweat trickle down my face and grow to large drops, forming pools of wet on the new aerobics floor. My eyes then focused on the all-too-telling mirror that revealed a pinched leotard and an exposed bra strap. What surprised me was my expression. The mirror reflected a tense face, rigid except for an occasional wince of pain and wisps of hair that escaped the taut headband.

I used to love to dance and sweat and do aerobics. But now I looked so grim! I looked like I wanted to punch someone—like I wanted to fight.

I was fighting. But who was I fighting? God? Myself? The rapist? The gossips? Victimization? An unfair world?

Again I turned to my reflection in the mirror. I was toned to the bone. And my bones were clearly visible. Three rows back, I could count my ribs.

The journey back to Massachusetts from California had taken its toll. Though I felt safer in my hometown, I had returned to sensational headlines: the Big Dan rape trial involving a gang rape on a pool table; the Holbrook Five trial of a group of teenagers accused of gang rape.

And then there was the nurse, Debby Smith.

Gruesome details of Debby's demise were revealed at the trial of her murderers and recounted in all the newspapers.

The evening shift at a local hospital had proved to be Debby's last. Exhausted from her night's labor, Debby had returned to her Commonwealth Avenue apartment in Boston to get a few hours of well-deserved sleep.

It was one o'clock on a sunny afternoon. While Debby slumbered, two burglars entered her apartment. Startled by a strange noise, she awoke to a knife against her throat. Quickly they blindfolded and then proceeded to disrobe her. In the struggle, the blindfold slipped.

"Open your eyes and you're dead," one of them growled.

In that split second of naked terror that only a victim can fathom, Debby blinked. And for probably the first time in his life, the robber kept his word. He slashed her throat.

There but for the blink of an eye . . .

I, too, was given that order. But my eyes were shut so tightly that I later had difficulty identifying the rapist at line-ups.

Debby blinked. I didn't. One small, involuntary, reflex action accomplished in a fraction of a second. Doing it caused Debby's demise. Not doing it saved my life.

Before I left California, my detective urged me to give the West Coast a second chance. He tried to tempt me by reading a New England weather report: May 10, and it was snowing in Boston.

"I'm a hearty New Englander, and I'm great at shoveling snow," I bragged. "I just can't handle looking into the barrel of a gun—and that's what happened to me in California. Well, those kinds of things just don't occur in Massachusetts."

Those words haunted me as I read the Boston papers. But I didn't respond to the terrifying tabloid headlines with fear. Instead I was furious. Rage, burning rage had replaced my terror.

I was to later learn that anger is a normal stage in the process of recovery. My psychiatrist claimed that I had already passed the first stages: shock, denial, and fear. Without realizing it, I was following each stage sequentially—most rape victims do. This is healthy; what is unhealthy is lingering over a stage or never completing it, never moving on.

People vary widely in the specific ways they navigate the stages of recovery. Sadly, some turn to alcohol or drugs to get rid of the fear and anger. Others alienate family and friends. Still others, like myself, get compulsive.

Even before the rape, a bad day at work never drove me to the bars to drink away my stress. Instead, I always exercised. So it wasn't surprising that I turned to aerobics and dance to get rid of the incredible anger that I felt. I took five or six classes a day. One time I figured that I had done a thousand jumping jacks in the course of a night.

Anger propelled me. It drove me to my home away from home—to the ubiquitous spot of the eighties that supplanted bars, singles' dances, gourmet clubs, and progressive dinners as "the place to be":

The health club.

In the beginning, there had been dark, dingy places called gyms, where men in ratty sneakers played basketball, punched each other playfully, and told off-color jokes. Few women were seen in these places. But the eighties saw the rise of the health clubs—carpeted spas sporting high-tech equipment, colorful decor, and juice bars. Men and women looked good as they worked out in two-hundred-dollar warmup suits and accessories.

It was the fad of the eighties—the fitness craze. But it was more than a fad. From America's beginnings, we had built a culture around our ability to shape our own destiny. Then, more recently, we had extended that effort to our own bodies. The "me" generation, with its relentless pursuit of personal fulfillment, had changed the essentially positive goal of physical fitness into the crusade of the decade. And it produced "aerobic types" like me, devoted to the gospel of the eighties: youth, beauty, thinness. Determined to be perfect.

Perfect. There was even a movie with this title as Hollywood and Madison Avenue joined hands to promote the faces and bodies they said we should all possess. The pursuit of perfection swelled the coffers of the fitness clubs and created new fanatics—and new victims. Each had his or her story.

There was Sally. Tall, slender, Nordic looking, and always smiling, she was everyone's favorite aerobics instructor. She really seemed to care about her students, and they idolized her. But Sally had her secret: "Two years ago I weighed two hundred pounds. I live in constant fear that I will lose control and get my old body back. You see, if I eat one cookie, I finish the whole box. So I keep an old picture of myself inside my tape case. I look at it often. It makes me exercise harder and longer."

And then there was Joanie. Quietly, almost furtively, she would enter the locker room. Her appearance was nondescript, except for her thin, almost emaciated frame. Usually, no one noticed her as she changed quickly, then slipped into the bathroom. Alone in the stall, she would stick a finger down her throat and make herself throw up. Then she would emerge, head down, and sullenly head for class.

Kathy would cloister herself in the far corner of the aerobics room. Ten to fifteen years older than the other class members, she tried valiantly to keep up with the young fillies who effortlessly lifted their limbs overhead. They were trying to avoid the beginning of cellulite. She was desperately fighting the clock—and considering a "tummy tuck."

"Control it." "Tough it out." "Let it burn." These were some of the colloquial expressions that shaped a decade and summed up a culture. Too often, sadly, that culture ended up twisting the real virtues of athletic endeavor—discipline, health, emotional release, and joy in God's gift of our bodies—into a narcissistic drive to overcome human imperfection.

I, too, was part of this culture. But after the rape, my priorities changed. Once driven to the pursuit of perfection, I was now using my physical workouts to maintain my sanity. My striving now became an expression of my will to live—a frantic quest to transcend the pain. The obsession with perfection, the competitive streak, the athletic test of mind and body now changed into a Herculean drive to handle my anger, to cope with life's unfair blows, to accept my fate, pick up the pieces, and go on living. I was, literally, dancing for my life!

"Come on, class. You can do it. Don't arch that back. Now we're going to add the arms. Flex it up! Swing it through and sweat it out."

Until I was soaking wet I couldn't stop exercising. Then, after about five hours, I limped to the locker room, stumbled into the shower, and trudged home, still clammy in new sweats—a somber silhouette against the flashy backdrop of the health club's neon sign.

I knew it was excessive. If gluttony was a sin, then five or six hours of aerobics had to be frowned on by the Almighty. And I admit I put my workouts even before my times of prayer and Bible study. But nothing else seemed to quell my anger. And strangely, my workouts and my quiet times with God seemed to work together.

Reading Scripture and praying always made me cry. In retrospect, I realize that this weeping was needed; a catharsis, a way of getting rid of the emotional pain. Aerobics was another form of catharsis, a way of working out my anger. And somehow aerobics gave me the courage to cry out to God.

In my Bible reading I focused on the Book of Job. And I noticed that Job questioned God for the first thirty-seven chapters, and God allowed him to rant and rave before answering. I, too, was candid with God and cried out to him. But I did my battle with God in aerobics class. My diatribe was done in rhythm, and my questions, accusations, and tirades were all done to the beat.

It would always happen in the middle of the class, when my body was in sync with the rhythm of the routine. My mind would turn to my predicament, and I would question God.

Why did this happen to me? What did I ever do to deserve such a fate? And God, where were you that night when I was being degraded? If you're a loving God, how could you look on while I was being tortured? Do you hear me, God? I need an answer.

Very often, amid high-impact kicks, jumping jacks, and triple turns, I would almost feel God's response. It was as if he waited until I was most vulnerable physically to mesh my acquired Scripture knowledge and prayerful pleas and give me an answer. It went something like this:

"Do fifty jacks. Out loud, counting down. Forty-nine . . . forty-eight . . .

God, you are all-powerful. You could have prevented it. I would have come to you eventually.

"Forty. Thirty-nine . . . thirty-eight . . ."

Susan, don't confuse God with life. Bad things happen to innocent people. Go on with your life. Go forward. Do good. It will make sense in time. It is not for you to know right now.

"Thirty. Twenty-nine . . . twenty-eight . . ."

But God, I'm so mad. I'm so angry. I can't forget. How can I go on?

"Twenty. Nineteen . . ."

Persevere. Like an athlete in training, now you feel the pain, the rigor, the hardship. But see the goal in sight—the goal attained.

One time during these exchanges, my shoelace became untied. It was just after a particularly stinging outburst, when I had screamed, *God, you're unfair. Why did you pick me to be raped? And if it had to happen, why didn't you just let me die?*

As I knelt down, crouching over the pesky lace, God seemed to answer, *Because I'm God and I'm sovereign. I wanted you to live, and you survived for a reason.*

At that moment, I was convicted. Bitter tears stung my face and wet my shoes. I remained kneeling while the dance class whirled around me.

This unorthodox form of prayer, which paired the physical and the spiritual, might appear irreverent on the surface. But on my knees I was too fearful to challenge God. On the dance floor we wrestled, and I vacillated between anger and praise.

I've heard it said that anyone who suffers swings back and forth emotionally. Job did. At one point he says to God, "Even if you slay me I will trust you." The next moment he is asking, "How could you let this happen to me?"

I alternately praised God for my survival and blamed him for the pain of memory that wouldn't subside.

The Bible is replete with examples of people who went through tough times and expressed their anger and frustration to God: David in his psalms, Jeremiah in his lamentations, and Elijah and Job. All were honest with God during their darkest hours.

For years, good counseling has advocated that the healthiest response to adversity is to acknowledge and express negative emotions such as anger instead of ignoring or denying them. The Bible also seems to promote this response. God wasn't shattered by the angry queries of his people in ancient times. They involved him in the process of overcoming their trials, and they emerged from their tirades with their faith intact.

The Bible also parallels the struggle of living a good life with that of an athlete. Several important passages compare and contrast spiritual strivings with athletic endeavors:

> In a race, everyone runs but only one person gets first prize. So run your race to win. To win the contest you must deny yourselves many things that would keep you from doing your best. An athlete goes to all this trouble just to win a blue ribbon or a silver cup, but we do it for a

heavenly reward that never disappears. So I run straight to the goal with purpose in every step. (1 Cor. 9:24–26 LB)

Not that I have already obtained all this, or have already been made perfect, but I press on to take hold of that for which Christ Jesus took hold of me. . . . Forgetting what is behind and straining toward what is ahead, I press on toward the goal to win the prize for which God has called me heavenward in Christ Jesus. (Phil. 3:12–14)

In retrospect, and in the light of further Bible study, perhaps my method for overcoming adversity wasn't so negative after all. I had one major point in common with my biblical predecessors. Though I questioned God, yelled at him, and challenged him, never once did I turn my back on him. God continued to be present in my healing process.

I continued with my excessive aerobics for quite awhile.

Then one day it happened—the nightmare of every dancer and athlete. Running for a bus, I tripped over a curb and fell. Excruciating pain shot through my left ankle. I had wrenched my foot in three places—the ankle bone, the instep, and the heel.

The doctor told me that I must stay off the foot completely for at least three weeks. Hopefully, I had just sprained it.

I thought that I would go insane. I was used to doing thirty-five hours of aerobics a week, and now—nothing. My feelings of stress noticeably increased. My insomnia returned. I felt like a caged animal. My temper flared often.

I thought my foot was better after two weeks, so I decided to return to class. I only intended to take one class my first day back. But the music was great, so I decided to go on to the second . . . and then the third.

That night, when I got home, I noticed a golf-ball-sized pocket of swelling on my left ankle. I iced it, then went to bed with a strange sense of foreboding.

I was to leave the next day on a grueling ten-day business trip. There would be no time for exercise. I cheered up, thinking that when I returned my ankle would be normal. But the swelling never healed, even when I had stopped dancing. And the pain was increasing.

I saw another doctor, who told me, "You probably have torn all the ligaments in your ankle. We can't tell with X-rays. We will have to operate. Your dancing days are over; that's for sure."

I was stunned. I sought another opinion.

"It looks like your ligaments are torn. We will have to go in arthroscopically and survey the damage. But you'll have to find a more sedentary hobby. How about sewing?"

This can't be. God, you can't take away my dance! What will I do? I need it. Why, I could talk to you in an aerobics dance class. That has to count for something!

I went from doctor to doctor. Eight in all. Though their methods of operating varied, the prognosis was the same:

"You will never dance again!"

Forgiveness: His Signature Piece

I t has been said that dance is the emblem of an era. Every decade ushers in a new dance genre—a signature piece that defines the times. The twenties, for example, had the Charleston; the thirties, the fox trot; the forties, the swing; and the fifties, the jitterbug. We reminisce about these periods through the music and the dances that seemed to shape their spirit. These art forms serve as historical cornerstones to jog our memories and dust off the cobwebs of years gone by.

Similarly, forgiveness is the cornerstone of Christianity—its signature piece. This foundation of forgiveness through the sacrificial, substitutionary atonement of Jesus Christ is what distinguishes it from other religions.

"I am the good shepherd. The good shepherd lays down his life for the sheep," said Jesus to his apostles.

God incarnate, virgin-born, sinless and spotless, Jesus Christ took on the burden of the sins of the world so that all might have eternal life. Apart from the death of Jesus, there can be no forgiveness.

Time after time, the theme of forgiveness dominated as Jesus met and spoke to the multitudes: the story of the prodigal son, the encounter with the adulterous woman at the well, the leper he healed, the thief hanging on the cross beside him, and—perhaps the most notable of the forgiven, Mary Magdalene.

A prostitute, an outcast, Mary seemed so far from the Son of God. But it is an irony that it was this sinner who lavished the greatest love on her Lord when she turned to him, washing his feet with her tears, drying them with her hair, anointing them with perfume. And it is probably no accident that the first he appeared to after his resurrection was Mary Magdalene.

We can forgive only to the degree that we have been forgiven. It is God's forgiveness of us that makes it possible for us to forgive others.

Charles Swindoll, in his book *Improving Your Serve*,[1] writes about a young seminarian he calls Aaron.

Aaron prayed that God would give him an important ministry—a position in a Christian organization or on some church staff. But as time passed, and no position appeared, Aaron realized he would have to take any job he could find to replenish his finances. The only position available was that of a bus driver on the South Side of Chicago. Aaron would be a rookie driver in a dangerous section of the city.

A gang of hoodlums quickly discovered the new driver and tried to intimidate him. Four days in a row, they got on and walked right past him without paying, despite his warnings.

The next day, the gang got on as usual. But Aaron saw a policeman on the corner, pulled over, and reported the incident. The officer boarded the bus and told the gang to pay or get off. They paid, but unfortunately the officer then disembarked. When the bus turned the corner, the gang attacked Aaron.

When Aaron came to, he was on the floor of the bus, bleeding profusely. Two teeth were missing, both eyes were swollen, and his money was missing. Anger, disillusionment, hurt, and resentment—all added fuel to the fire of his intense physical suffering. He wrestled with God for an answer.

Why did this happen? Where is God in all this? I wanted to serve him. I prayed for a ministry. I was willing to do anything . . . and this is the thanks I get!

Aaron decided to press charges. With the aid of the officer who had encountered the ruffians, most were rounded up and taken to the county jail. A hearing was scheduled.

When Aaron walked into the courtroom on the day of the hearing, the thugs glared at him, seething with anger. But as he looked at them, something strange happened. Suddenly he was seized with new thoughts and compassionate feelings. His heart went out to the boys who had abused him. Instead of hating them, he pitied them. They needed help, not more hate.

When a verdict of guilty was offered, Aaron surprised the courtroom when he asked permission to speak.

"Your honor, I would like you to total up all the days of punishment for these men—all the time sentenced—and I request that you allow me to go to jail in their place."

The courtroom was stunned.

Aaron turned and looked at the gang members and said, "It is because I forgive you."

The judge finally spoke, "Young man, you're out of order. This sort of thing has never been done before!" To which Aaron replied with the genius of inspiration, "Oh, yes it has, Your Honor. It happened over nineteen centuries ago, when a man from Galilee paid the penalty that all mankind deserved."

Aaron was not granted his request, but he did visit the gang members in prison. He led most of them to faith in Christ. And he began working with other street kids in South-Side Chicago. A ministry—the very thing that he had prayed for—evolved from the pain of abuse and assault.

To forgive. It's such a small, concise phrase—nine letters. It sounds so simple, but it is so difficult to do. For someone who has been hurt badly, it feels like an impossibility.

For me, forgiveness was the hardest requirement of my new Christian life. Scarred and deeply wounded by all that had happened, I responded to my pain by escaping into excessive activity. I was left injured, still broken, and desperate for the peace and serenity that eluded me.

Unforgiveness. Frozen anger coiled in bitterness and resentment. It is as stifling as a muffled scream, a voiceless cry. It is an awesome feeling of helplessness and hurt, a trapped feeling worse than death itself.

Encased in an ugly shell of unforgiveness, I was miserable. The aftermath of rape had left schisms in my relationships. It had left me livid toward the rapist and filled with debilitating hate for all criminals. And deep within, submerged in guilt, I still felt anger toward God.

I was now at an impasse. I had reached a crossroads in my walk with Christ. It was as if the Master had choreographed me into a corner and, to move upstage, I had to choose a direction. I could be angry and follow a stormy path. Or I could forgive.

I chose forgiveness. I had thrown all my "larger than life" questions at the Lord, and now I was ready to give up control. I would let God be God.

Jesus, I still don't understand why this happened to me or how it fits in with your plan for my life. I know that someday I

*will know your higher purpose. Until then, you are God; I am
the servant. And I forgive all.*

Forgiveness is not normal; it is superhuman. It is one
of those rare instances in life when the divine meets the
earthly, when God's power meshes with frail humanity
and God is glorified.

But some, like myself, have to hit bottom before they
will let God help them forgive. I reached the point where
it was either God or despair, the peace of forgiveness or
the relentless disharmony of an unforgiving spirit.

But it still seemed impossible. If I were to truly forgive
the rapist, I had to believe that if he asked God for forgiveness he would end up in heaven right beside me. I
knew that he was locked up three thousand miles away.
I knew he was receiving earthly punishment. That was
enough. My thoughts of revenge harmed only me.

Again, I had to let go, to give him to God. And in an act
of obedience, I had to choose to forgive him even if my
emotions still pointed in the other direction.

I frankly admit that this didn't happen overnight. It
was a process of God working in me, and speaking to me
through certain people he brought into my life, through
the stories they told.

One story was about the "black hole." That is how
they describe solitary confinement. Intent on restraining
and at times even breaking a man, it is the most dreaded
form of prison punishment. In total isolation, some die.
Many go mad.

Concerned about this, a kind man from my church
wanted to visit a man locked in solitary and reach out to
him with the love of Christ. With permission from the
prison chaplain, he entered the black hole. He describes
the scene:

"The stench knocks you out—a putrid combination of
sweat, urine, and mildew. On the grimy grey walls were

blotches of peeling paint; a filthy, roach-infested floor served as a resting area for the meek-looking, bespectacled man in front of me. He seemed so harmless; it was difficult to believe he had caused such trouble among the inmates.

"I had planned to discuss a Bible passage with the gentleman, but he pre-empted our study by telling me that he had accepted Jesus as Lord and that he knew Christ forgave him for all his sins, including the crime that had sent him to prison."

"You see," he explained, "I molested my thirteen-year-old stepdaughter. But I know in my heart that Jesus has forgiven me."

"I was sickened," my friend continued. "I also no longer wanted to help this man." Feeling guilty, my friend approached the prison chaplain and related the afternoon's events.

"I can understand how you feel. But let's try something. Close your eyes for a minute. Now picture Jesus on Calvary, and see yourself before the cross. Realize that he is suffering for your sins. Now, standing beside you, also before the cross, is the inmate you just visited. Before the cross, all are equal, and all sins have been forgiven."

The next day, the man from my church returned to the black hole to visit the inmate again.

More help came from a testimony I heard one night at a church gathering from a former prisoner. This man was sent to jail for a year on trumped-up charges. He questioned God about his circumstances but came to the conclusion that Jesus had a plan in all that had happened to him. A Christian before entering the penitentiary, he worked with a chaplain to set up Bible studies throughout the prison. These meetings were amazingly successful in conveying God's forgiveness to his fellow prisoners.

After this man had spent a year of his life incarcerated, the charges were dropped and he was freed.

The conclusion to this man's testimony—his vision of forgiveness—still resounds in me. He said, "The final stage of forgiveness is to give away a part of yourself—reaching out to others with love and acceptance. What one person does for another is what's going to ignite and impact a whole people. So get outside yourself. And forgive."

Something else about that man's testimony helped me move toward forgiveness. He was black. The man who raped me was black, too. And though I had solid relationships with black friends from church and work, seeing young blacks in garb similar to what my assailants had worn that night brought out a fear I couldn't control.

But God worked my fear out of me in a truly miraculous way.

Crippled by my ankle injury and distraught over the doctors' prognosis, I had given up any hope of recovery when a friend recommended a doctor who was a basketball player, a skier, a consummate athlete. He had studied in Switzerland and had operated on injured members of the Olympic ski team.

I figured that one more visit couldn't hurt. After all, this would up the tally to nine doctor bills.

But this doctor was different. Instantly we enjoyed the mutual respect and rapport of fellow athletes. He understood how important dance and aerobics were to me.

The prognosis?

The operation would be painful, the recovery long. But there was a chance that I could dance again.

I felt totally safe in my new doctor's hands. I was sure he was sent from God. He was gentle, soft-spoken, compassionate, brilliant . . . and black.

I had been brutalized and raped by black ruffians. Now God in his wisdom and providential care saw to it that a talented black doctor would put me back together again.

My torn ligaments would be fused by the hand of man, but healed by the touch of God.

That night I prayed the prayer of relinquishment:

Jesus, you are Lord of every area of my life. I surrender all to you, including my injured foot and my beloved dance. I put this operation in your hands, and I leave the outcome to you. If you give me my foot back, I will try to find a way to use it for your glory. Whatever you decide, I will accept.

The date for the operation was set. The doctor gave me a brace to wear. It held what was left of my foot in place.

The day before the operation, he checked me over one more time.

"Don't eat or drink anything—even water—after midnight. And you should be at the hospital by ten in the morning."

I had a sudden thought.

"Doctor, if I ran or even danced while wearing this brace, could I further damage this foot?"

"No, all the ligaments are torn already. You couldn't damage it any further. . . . Why do you ask?"

"Oh . . . no reason."

The night before the operation, I just pretended I was going on a trip. I packed and primped—doing my nails, soaking in a bubble bath, catering to myself to avoid reality. But I awoke the next morning with a strange sense of foreboding.

What if the operation didn't work? What if I got worse? What if. . . .

I took the brace from the nightstand and buckled its awkward straps to my calf, tightly securing my ankle region.

I stomped awkwardly to the other room, searching frantically for the blue-and-white monstrosity that contained a huge part of my life: my workout bag. Rifling through its contents like a woman possessed, I gave no thought to style or color—or even matching socks. Somehow I got dressed, then ventured out into the cold November morning, pulling my parka over my skimpy attire.

My car stalled again and again. But still I wouldn't give up.

With breakneck speed I pulled into the parking lot.

I waved the customary card in front of the receptionist.

Stripping off my heavy winter coat, I stopped suddenly and looked up.

Father, forgive me, for I do know what I'm doing. . . ."

"Hi, Susan. Want a sip of water?" A friend handed me her water bottle.

"No thanks," I responded. "I'm fasting."

I had decided to take an early-morning aerobics class before the operation. Yes, it was crazy. But my doctor had said I couldn't do any more harm. And I had resigned myself to a long recovery and made peace with God about the possibility that this might be my last dance.

Ten minutes before the end of class, I grabbed my workout bag and hurried home. A quick shower, and then my girlfriend had arrived to take me to the hospital. There was no time for nerves.

Admission was accomplished in record time, and before I knew it, I was donning a strange, green, loose-fitting garment worn, I am told, during some operations. They even had matching green paper slippers for my wheelchair ride down to the operating room.

In pre-op they moved me to a gurney, and a nurse monitored my vital signs. Then, with less than twenty minutes to go, they wheeled me into the operating room.

My doctor and several other medical personnel, also attired in hospital green, swarmed around me, each performing his or her particular task on various parts of my anatomy.

"We're going to give you a shot to make you sleepy before we finally put you out with anesthetic," said my doctor.

I felt the prick, then I started feeling very drowsy and mellow. All that green was becoming blurry. But I could still hear their pre-op chatter.

"Oh, no!" someone in green exclaimed. "We're in trouble. She has toenail polish on all ten toes."

So much for my primping the night before. I didn't realize that scrubbing for an operation included taking off nail polish as well.

I felt myself going under. But before I did, I found my doctor's hand and grabbed it. I raised my heavy eyelids, and the last words my parched mouth uttered were, "Sorry. I was just trying to be well groomed."

I held up the operation for two hours.

New Steps for a New Life

ever since I can remember, I have loved to dance. In old home movies I can be seen dancing my way into the hearts of any one who would watch and applaud, often eclipsing my younger brother who stared in drooling wonder at such boldness.

One day, at the tender age of six, I was flipping the television dial, and suddenly there they were. In an empty ballroom dominated by a crystal globe that refracted the light and scattered it across the stage were two glamorous creatures. Elegantly they glided into my living room, changing my life forever.

Fred and Ginger.

The mere mention of this dazzling duo conjures up images of class, style, finesse—a perfect blend of music and movement.

Whirling through a celluloid eternity of magic, Astaire and Rogers piqued the imagination of a star-struck child. With rapt attention I studied their long-limbed command of rhythm and space, their use of eloquent gestures to render so vividly the splendor of romantic love.

It was an excursion into enchantment.

And I was easily enchanted! I spent hours in front of the mirror, mimicking the moves of the masters and dreaming of the day when I, too, would dance with distinction.

Dance has existed since the beginning of time as ritual, as recreation, as spectacle, as custom, and even as worship. The Bible is replete with examples of how dance is used to offer praise and thanksgiving to God. In fact, dance is mentioned frequently in the Bible:

> You turned my wailing into dancing. (Ps. 30:11)

> David . . . danced before the LORD with all his might. (2 Sam. 6:14)

> Praise him with the harp and lyre,
> Praise him with tambourine and dancing. (Ps. 150:3–4)

Many famous choreographers have commented on the spiritual side of dance:

> "In a dancer's body, we as audience must see ourselves— something of the miracle that is a human being, motivated, disciplined, concentrated," said Martha Graham.

> Twyla Tharp has said, "Dance represents the God in me."

> "Only God can create. Man can only assemble what is out there," claimed ballet choreographer George Balanchine.

> "Dance is worship," said Agnes deMille.[1]

Simply put, dance is a very high art. Dancers wordlessly demonstrate, using only their bodies, every facet of human emotion. Dance inspires and transforms the commonplace. It can transport both dancer and audience into another world—a world of transcendent wonder and beauty.

But dance is also tremendously physical—an athletic endeavor. To dance well requires that all aspects of a person—mind, spirit, and body—work in concert. That "whole person" involvement was one of the things I loved most about dance. It is art done by an athlete.

And it was that "athlete" angle that occupied my attention one long afternoon. I sat sprawled in my chair, with my foot in its heavy cast propped up in front of me, watching a movie on TV. It was that wonderful old musical, *Singin' in the Rain*, starring one of my favorite dancers, Gene Kelly.

If Fred Astaire was the 1930s' sine qua non of suave, then Gene Kelly electrified the 1940s with a daring, athletic dance style that became his hallmark. Muscular and casual in a striped T-shirt, a sailor suit, or even a raincoat, Kelly managed to imbue every number with a sense of powerful grace. And with his crooked grin and midwest accent, he managed to communicate that dance is for everybody, not just "artistic types."

Kelly's dance style was rooted in his lifelong belief that dancing and athletics were inextricably linked. In 1956, in a television series titled *Dancing: A Man's Game*, he set out to illustrate that conviction. Assembling a few of the world's greatest sportsmen for the series, Kelly showed that most dance movements have their athletic equivalent on the gym floor or playing field. And he maintained that the only difference between sport and dancing is that one is competitive and the other is creative.

Gene Kelly, with his emphasis on combining athletics and dance, foreshadowed the eighties, when a new blend of dance steps and cardiovascular training became the rage. Dancers were among the first to recognize that their art fit the requirements of aerobic conditioning beautifully and that adding routines and music to a workout made it much more enjoyable for most people. Instructors began to put

together dance routines designed to enhance cardiovascular fitness, and people flocked to the classes. I eagerly
joined the fray.

For me, aerobic dance combined the best of both
worlds—my enchantment with dance and my competitive athletic streak. The dance, with its complexly choreographed steps, satisfied my yen for variety, while the sus-
tained energy level required (the "aerobic" part) gave me
a natural athletic high which made me break out in a
smile during class. This used to catch the eye of my
teachers. They didn't always know my name, but they
knew me as "the one who smiles" in a class where everyone else was grimacing. Dance and movement always
gave me such joy.

"I'm singin' . . . and dancin' . . . in the rain," crooned
Gene Kelly from my TV. He swung around a lamppost
with such infectious *joie de vivre* that I longed to jump up
and join him. But my eyes wandered once again from the
screen to the cast, a grim reminder of reality.

I was home from the hospital, off work on two months'
medical leave. I whiled away the time watching old Hollywood musicals and wondering whether I would ever dance
again. I had endless hours for reflection and introspection.

The movie ended; I clicked it off. I shifted uncomfort-
ably—what next?

Listlessly I picked up a cassette album from the table
next to me, the gift of a visiting colleague who thought it
would inspire me. I selected a tape at random, dropped it
in the player, pushed the "Start" button . . . and experienced the first in a cascade of surprises.

I knew that voice—from long ago! Time, which often
dulls the lustre of memories, graciously took a holiday as I
sat there listening, and my mind turned back the clock . . .

When I was an energetic, exuberant child, there was
never a sign that I would be singled out for any particular

dramatic experience in life. I do remember, though, that I yearned for an exciting future. Sometimes at night, gazing at the stars, I felt certain that something extraordinary was going to happen to me. I had one surpassing goal: I did not want to be ordinary.

I attended a Catholic primary school with three of my cousins. Linda was in my grade, and our big cousins Mike and Billy were two and three grades older. They called us the little brats and vacillated between protecting us and playing practical jokes.

Just before Christmas, Mike and Bill and their friend Tom took me aside and said, "Sister Francis Mary is going to ask if you know any Christmas carols, and we are going to teach you one so that you will be Sister's favorite."

I eagerly listened and memorized the words.

Next day in class, Sister asked us first-graders, "Children, does anyone know the words to a Christmas carol?"

I was the only one to raise my hand.

"Susan, which carol do you know?"

"'The First Noel,' Sister."

"Well, why don't you sing it for the class?"

Concentrating on the words I had been taught, I belted out, "Noel, Noel, Noel, Noel. We ain't got no water 'cause we ain't got no well."

Sister Francis Mary kept me after school till Easter.

The boys thought it was hysterical—especially Tom. This was one of their worst practical jokes. But I would get them. I vowed revenge, as only a six-year-old can.

I got my chance the next day. We were all playing a game of hide-and-seek. Linda and I had to choose whether we wanted to be on Mike or Billy's team. Fickle and finicky, we both said we wanted Mike. Tom turned to me and said, "If you choose Billy, you'll be my best friend."

"Who cares," I snapped triumphantly.

My mother, it seemed, came out of nowhere and smacked me. "Couldn't you be nice to that boy and do what he asked?"

Tom corrected her, "Don't punish her. She treats me like Mike and Bill. I like that."

Let me tell you what has since happened to Tom. He is a film and television actor, a world-class athlete who holds two national championship records in wrestling, a musician, an author. He earned a degree at Harvard in clinical psychology. He runs six miles a day. He skydives (with thirty-seven jumps on his record). He swims. And he's blind.

Tom has been blind since childhood. But he refused to be a victim. He participated in normal childhood games, including playing hide-and-seek with fresh little girls.

When I was in college, one night a group of friends went to a club to hear a new musician. I tagged along and discovered that debuting musician was Tom. During intermission I went up and reintroduced myself. To my chagrin he blurted out, "Oh yeah, the little brat."

Trying desperately to cover my embarrassment I asked, "Tom, how far do you plan to go with your music and writing?"

"Right to the top!" was his instant reply.

The tape that I was listening to was my childhood friend Tom. He was addressing a Million Dollar Roundtable of five thousand insurance executives from around the world. The title of his speech: "Turning Your Disadvantage into an Advantage."

"You've got a disadvantage? Take advantage of it. People don't buy similarity; they buy differences," Tom's voice on the tape advised.

"That disadvantage is what makes you different—unique. Have you ever considered the impact your disadvantage would have on the world if you got out of your self-pity, took life by the throat, and became a message?

"What is your story?" asked Tom. "Everybody has a story. And most likely, there is some injustice in it. You think that's the thing that has caused you to become a failure. But I'm here to tell you it could very possibly be your message for life."[2]

I sat in rapt attention. Despite Tom's remarkable talents, he probably wouldn't have an audience if he were not blind. This fact struck a responsive chord.

I felt that I, too, had a message. My life had changed radically since the rape. After all, it was the reason I came to Jesus. And my growing relation with him gave my testimony a dimension that Tom's lacked.

But since the attack I had been existing in a survival mode: surviving the rape, surviving a breakdown, surviving in my career, and now trying to survive this operation and regain my dancing feet.

Like Henry Wadsworth Longfellow, I believed "that nothing is accidental with the Lord." God had a plan for my life, and it had to include more than survival. Perhaps he was creating the background for the tapestry of my life, weaving the many dark threads to set off the color of his design.

With my plaster cast plopped unceremoniously on the coffee table, I put aside my video and audio pursuits to catch up on my reading. From the stack beside me I chose *The Hiding Place* by Corrie ten Boom. Though I knew the story of this Dutch woman's rescue of thousands of Jews and her subsequent internment in a concentration camp, I had never actually read her book.

I was enthralled with the courage and the faith shown by Corrie and her family in the face of impending doom. One particular part of the story vivified me.

Caught harboring Jews in their home, the ten Boom family were taken to gestapo headquarters. Alone with one gestapo official, Corrie offered him her Christian testimony. He ridiculed her and sent her away, but the next day he sent for her again. He said, "I wasn't able to sleep last night thinking about what you said. There is time enough for the questioning. Tell me all you know about Jesus."

Next, Betsy, Corrie's sister, entered for her inquisition. With great joy she testified to her faith, then she said, "It is important to speak about Jesus, but it is more important to speak to him. Would you allow me to pray with you?" He agreed. Corrie described that scene many years later: "There they were—the prisoner with her judge—the victim with her victimizer."[3]

As I read those words, something stirred inside me—a sudden rush, a kaleidoscope of thoughts, feelings, fragmentary phrases from what I had read and heard: *Victim and victimizer . . . prisoner . . . prison . . . testimony . . . message . . . pray . . . changed lives . . . disadvantage . . . make a difference. . . .*

Then it came to me. *Prison.* I could go into prison, like that man in my church, and work with criminals—not only to be sure I had forgiven, but to tell them my story. I could bring them the message of the gospel and assure them that people really can change.

But doubt dampened my rising excitement. Why would they listen to me? From their point of view I was still well off, successful, from another world. What would we really have in common?

Discouraged, I picked up my book again. But snippets from Tom's tape kept swirling around in my head: *Your disadvantage. . . . Use it. . . . It makes you unique. . . . It is your message.*

Tom's disadvantage was his blindness. Mine was the rape and my subsequent struggle with fear and anger.

But what was my unique message?

Then it came to me—another epiphany. I had told God that if he gave me my foot back, I would find a way to use it for him. Now I knew how.

I could teach aerobic dance in a women's prison and use it as a platform for the gospel message.

Dance, exercise, and aerobics could be common denominators, shared interests. Also, a good instructor can make exercise fun. If I could do that, I could help foster good relationships and show prisoners what it is like to be a joyful Christian.

My exuberance was suddenly tempered once again, this time by the throbbing of my foot in its plaster prison, bringing me back to the real world of the moment.

Lord, I know this idea is from you. But how can I accomplish it if I can't dance? Are you going to heal me?

Jesus said, "With God all things are possible" (Matt. 19:26). And I figured that if God could evangelize the then known world with fishermen and tax collectors, then he can start a dance ministry with a cripple.

"Do not despise this small beginning, for the eyes of the Lord rejoice to see the work begin," says God's Word (Zech. 4:10 LB). But after this revelation of my ministry, I returned to work for weeks on crutches. Then came a brace, and finally a cane. I was now described as "the one who limps."

I went to physical therapy three times a week for longer than I care to remember. But ever so slowly the pain subsided, the limp lessened, and I graduated from orthopedic shoes to respectable flats.

One day I walked into the doctor's office for my usual visit. He proceeded with his routine manipulations of my foot while I yawned with boredom. Then I realized he had spoken to me.

"You're ready."

"Ready for what?" I inquired.

"To go back."

"Back where?" I was puzzled.

My usually shy, reserved doctor took me by the shoulders, looked me in the eye, and said, "Dance, girl. That's why we operated."

. I couldn't believe it. Praise the Lord!

Of course, I wouldn't know, until I tried, what my limitations were. Maybe I would never get a full range of motion back, or I would have too much pain. But I was determined to get in there and try. I made immediate plans to join my favorite dance troupe at the next available class.

The day came. I was psyched. I walked into the studio and there it was—the sweet, familiar smell of sweat. That night I wouldn't have traded it for Parisian perfume. I strutted to the center of the locker room and announced at the top of my lungs, "I'm back."

Shrieks. Giggles. Hugs. Dancing friends swarmed around me with various renditions of "Welcome back!"

"We've missed you."

"Wait till you see our new numbers!"

"Was it very painful?"

"Laid up all that time, and you didn't gain any weight!"

"You look rested, peaceful. Are you ready to really work out?"

I didn't know the answer to that one yet. But I was about to find out.

I slipped the athletic brace under my foot, wincing slightly. Quickly, I tied my shoes as I heard the music starting.

"I've been saving your spot," said my good friend Lori, smiling. We always danced beside each other.

I took my place beside her and then turned to the teacher. "Let's dance to some of the old tunes. I want to see if I've still got it," I joked.

She humored me. And I was in a state of euphoria. My foot felt strained, but there was no real pain. I thanked God profusely. I went home and iced my foot and rested. But I also made plans to get together with the women from my church who were interested in my prison dance ministry.

We started meeting once a week, choreographing numbers that we thought the prisoners would enjoy. We also discussed the format of the class. We would start with aerobics set to popular tunes, then cool down with Christian music, and finally end with a fifteen-minute segment of prayer and sharing. We decided that we would be ready to go into prison by the end of January. We made contact with the outreach ministries of our church, and they prepared the inmates for our imminent arrival.

I was excited. Only one thing was troubling me. What would we call our group? If we took on the same name as our church, I thought we might intimidate nonbelievers who otherwise might be interested in an aerobics program.

Then, during my morning devotions, it came to me. There it was in God's Word—my story, what Jesus had done for me: "You have turned my sadness into a joyful dance" (Ps. 30:11).

And he had. Only a loving God could create a ministry out of adversity. And only a gracious God would allow me to serve him doing what gave me so much joy—dance!

We would call ourselves The Joy Dancers.

Since we had already decided to wear big T-shirts to work out, we would have "Joy Dancers" inscribed on the front. And on the back would be those wonderful words from Psalm 30: "You have turned my sadness into a joyful dance."

Name decided. Costumes ready. Everything in place. Curtain up!

Enter the Joy Dancers

Barbed Wire:

Razor-ribbon. Replica of restraint. Steely reminder of quarantine. Muted but malevolent mechanism of coiled confinement.

It was 25 January 1989—a bitter-cold winter night. The barbed wire encircling the compound glistened as strands of icicles hung precipitously from its spirals. I shivered as I maneuvered my car up the long driveway. Police cars were lined up in columns, and guards walked briskly through the yard tightly holding the leashes of sinister-looking canines.

Why did I ever think this was going to work? What a lousy way to spend a Thursday night after a hard day of work. I must be crazy!

I turned off the ignition and tightened my jacket around my chest to hide the trembling. I said to my companions, "Let's say a quick prayer. We still have some time."

We joined hands and I began, "Lord, we have to confess that we're really scared. I thought this was such a great idea for a ministry, but now I'm not so sure. Lord, none of us has ever been inside of a prison, and we don't know what to expect. But we do believe that you will be with us. After all, we're here for you. We stand on your Word, which says, 'I was in prison and you came to visit me' [Matt. 25:36]. Help us to bring the good news of the gospel to these women. And through our aerobics program, let us bring them an hour of good clean fun and healthy exercise once a week."

We hugged each other, got out of the car, walked past the police and the dogs. We entered a smoky, crowded area inhabited with scruffy-looking individuals.

All prison proceedings came to an abrupt halt, and all eyes were on us—six pony-tailed women with pink headbands, matching leg warmers, aerobic shoes, and startling, colorful T-shirts adorned with black script.

"What do you call yourselves?" asked the guard.

"The Joy Dancers."

I turned around to show him my back.

"You have turned my sadness into a joyful dance," he read. "What's that from?"

"The Bible. It's Scripture."

"I've never read the Bible. In fact, that's the first Scripture I've ever read," he responded.

"Bring in the aerobics people to get searched," bellowed the woman guard from the anteroom.

We entered a small enclosed area—the trap, they called it.

Two large female guards faced us and ordered us up against the wall. One guard focused on one of my fellow instructors.

"Do you have a weapon in your pocket? What is that sticking out?"

"It's . . . my . . . hipbone," she stuttered.

The guards looked at each other and burst out laughing.

"We don't see many hipbones around here," she volunteered. Their faces seemed to soften, and the rest of the search went smoothly.

"Extend your arms to the side. Now open your mouth. Lift up your right foot. Now left.

"Do you plan to have a hole in your sock every week?"

I looked down. Peering through the pink terry cloth was my big toe. My face matched my socks.

We passed inspection, and as the guard turned the key admitting us into the jail she offered, "It will get easier each time. Trust me." She then pressed a buzzer and yelled, "Six for the front."

Clutching our aerobics tapes, pulling up our leg warmers, and fastening our headbands, we entered . . . prison.

Lock, double-lock. Keys clanking all the way. We followed the guard down a long hall deep into the recesses of the institution. He turned left and opened the door to a large, musty gym where sixty women prisoners waited.

Walking to the front of the room was like running the gauntlet. Inmates awaited us with arms folded, jaws set, and a defiant stance that challenged our very existence. They looked us up and down, and we overheard a host of comments and dares.

"Look at them. What do those shirts say?"

"Joy Dancers? Get real."

"They're from church. What can these church girls show us?"

"We're all cued up. Now let's do it just as we rehearsed."

Lord, it's all yours.

"Hi. We're the Joy Dancers. We've put together an aer-obic dance program that we hope is both fun and great exercise. Our songs are based on top-forty hits, and then we use Christian music during our cooldown. We also pray at the very end, and tonight we will ask God to heal any aching muscles. Next week I'll give you a copy of the Dancer's Prayer, and that is how we will begin class. Don't worry if you can't get all the steps tonight, because we'll be here every week. Is everybody ready?"

Expectant hush.

"Hit it."

"Walk front. Touch left and clap."

"Oh, I love this song. These church girls can really move."

"Now we're going to learn a new dance. First combi-nation looks like this. Okay, let's try it."

"Great job, everybody!"

"Hey, what's going on in here?"

"No problem, Sergeant. We're just dancing."

Lord, they like it. They like the program. It's working. Be with me when I pray. Give me your words.

"All right, time to cool down. Listen to the words of this song and keep your movements slow and fluid."

When you pray and you call out his name,
    He hears you . . .[1]

"Now, everyone, please bow your head. You there in the back row, bow your head.

"Dear Lord, thank you for our time together tonight. I ask that you protect these women, who are precious in your sight. Let them know, Lord, that they are loved with an everlasting love, and that always underneath are your everlasting arms. And Father, help them to realize that when they call out to you, you do hear them. They don't have to say specific prayers, but rather just talk to you like a Father—because you do care and you do understand. And you do forgive. All we have to do is ask.

"And, Lord, I ask that you somehow let them know that no matter what they've done—regardless of how bad it is—that you will forgive them. And I just pray that with your help—and a little help from Ben Gay ointment—that you will bring them back next week so that they, too, can be Joy Dancers.

"That's class. Thanks for coming. God bless you."

Like a scene from a movie, sixty women swarmed around us, hugging and praising all the instructors.

The guards looked on in wonder.

This time we didn't mind hearing the comments.

"This is the best thing we've ever had here. Are you really coming back next week?"

"That was a really beautiful prayer. Does Jesus really forgive anything?"

"I loved the dances."

"Your shirts are cool. Are you going to get some for us? We want to be Joy Dancers."

Enjoying all the kudos, I barely noticed the three women who gradually stalked me and finally surrounded me. I was cut off from the rest of the class and the other instructors.

Oh, Lord, I know I was warned about this. Please protect me.

One woman, the ringleader, moved nearer, eyeing me suspiciously. When she was so close that I could count the tiny beads of sweat on the grooves of her face, she halted, pointed a bony index finger at me, and said, "You dance real good for a white girl!"

I left there on cloud nine. I felt that if I died that night I would hear God's words, "Well done, good and faithful servant."

It was just the beginning. As the weeks wore on, we became more involved with the women as they confided in us and asked us to pray for their particular needs. We did have our difficult times and difficult individuals. Some we won over, some we didn't.

The night of our second class, a burly woman with a shorn skull entered the gym. She scrutinized me with disgust and then voiced her opinion for everyone to hear.

"This broad will never last in here. She looks like a wimp. Three, four weeks max, and then she'll go crying back to the suburbs and figure she's done her one good deed in life."

With a sardonic smile, she folded her arms decisively and swaggered away.

Months later she approached me again.

"I've got to hand it to you, you're a lot tougher than you look. I get a kick out of watching you. You really love doing this, and it shows. You look like a happy, excited little kid. And when we watch you and dance with you, we start feeling that way too, even if it is just for an hour."

Another night, a rowdy group of women came in and took over. They wouldn't let us put the tapes in the recorder/radio. They were playing the radio, singing, snapping their fingers, and sashaying around the gym as if it was their turf.

"Let's get out of here," said one of my instructors. "They want trouble."

One prisoner grabbed my tapes and then sat up on the table with the recorder, hugging it possessively. She leaned back slowly, her eyes narrowing, her lips drawn back sourly to expose a glistening gold tooth.

"Just what do you plan to do in here tonight?"

"Dance. We do choreographed routines to music."

"Is that church music?"

"No. You know that song that's playing on the radio right now that you seem to like so much? Well, that is on our tape. And choreography is putting dance steps to a whole song, like you see on TV. Why don't you try it? You might like it. Would you mind putting my tape in the recorder?"

"Why not! I got nothing better to do."

"You can stand right in back of me, and then you can learn the steps to your favorite song!"

Extending a thin flexed arm, she motioned for the rest of her gang to fall in line.

They stayed for the whole class, even the prayer.

But they never came back.

As the weeks wore on, I discovered that most of these women had been harming their bodies with drugs and alcohol and had been mistreated by pimps and drug dealers. Some had been molested by family members, often since early childhood. No matter what the crime, most had one thing in common—they were filled with self-hate. Their bodies were things to be used and abused.

The prison chaplain had told me that before I could come in there proclaiming to these women that Jesus loved them, I had to teach them to love themselves. A good place to start was with a healthy respect for the body—the temple of the soul.

Enter the Joy Dancers.

Tales of the Dance

My purpose in beginning the Joy Dancers was twofold. First, I wanted to establish a common ground for communication—sharing the gospel. Second, I wanted to provide an outlet for the prisoners' anger, stress, and violent propensities and at the same time to give them a better self-image.

Each week, I hoped, as they got into better shape, they would become more attuned to their own physicality and achieve a sense of accomplishment as they learned new dance routines. Their health would also benefit as their heart rates improved, their blood pressure and cholesterol levels normalized, and the pounds began to come off. (A month after my first class, some of the inmates began doing aerobics on their own twice a week.)

I quickly learned just how deep these women's physical needs really were. For ladies in their late teens and early twenties, they were in terrible shape. I could see the effects of drugs on both mind and body. Many had trouble following even a very simple routine, and initially the forty-five-minute workouts we had planned were too much for them.

One night, as I was leading the second song, I happened to glance over my shoulder. Most of the women were already sitting in chairs around the gym, huffing and puffing. So we had to revamp our whole program, switching to easier movements and slower songs until they had built some endurance.

Excess weight was also a problem for most of these women. A combination of inactivity, greasy prison food, and the absence of unhealthy drugs usually filled them out considerably. This contributed to their depression and poor body image.

But after a few weeks, we began to hear glowing reports about the weight they were losing, the steps they had perfected. Several told us they intended to continue with aerobics after they were freed. And after a while, they began bringing requests for the prayer time after our workout. Gradually, we began to see inmates make new commitments to both their physical and spiritual well being.

Most of the prisoners were more than willing to work at the program for one reason—they loved to dance. So did we. We all shared a common love of music and movement. Dance brought inmates and instructors together—having fun, refining the craft, building our strength and endurance. And whenever people are getting together for good purposes, that's a sign that God is at work.

As our classes continued, other benefits became apparent. For instance, we were able to introduce many of these women to a dancer's discipline—the discipline of a chorus line and a ballet *barre*. Most inmates' dancing experience consisted of a few rap steps with no particular sequence or choreography. We taught them to memorize steps and routines and to move together in concert with others. These were disciplines that could be carried over into other areas of their lives.

As I had hoped, our classes provided an emotional out-let for women who lived under constant stress. Feeling confined, angry, hopeless, and bitter, many inmates entered my class with skepticism—some with an attitude. I quickly came to recognize the many kinds of pain that lay behind their words and actions.

Anger. The acid of anger is perhaps the most powerful emotion there is. It courses through a body burning and destroying any positive emotion that tries to surface. Anger exists for a reason. It is a signal, a message that we are being hurt, our rights are being violated, our needs aren't being met, our desires or ambitions are being thwarted.

There is nothing wrong with anger as an emotion; even the Bible says, "Be angry." But then it adds, "But do not sin" (Eph. 4:26). The problem with anger is not its exis-tence, but its expression. And that's where so many of the women in our class got in trouble. They had no outlet for their inevitable anger—at their families, at the prison sys-tem, at society, at themselves. Most of them also had no positive models for handling anger. No wonder they lashed out!

I understood all too well the power of anger. There had been times after the rape when my rage almost got out of control. But when I got angry I always headed straight for the treadmill or the Stairmaster to quell my fury. I hit the exercise machines. Many inmates hit someone else. The anger was the same; what differed was the means of man-aging the anger.

My commitment was to teach the women to turn anger into a constructive force for reshaping their lives—to

channel it into something that would benefit them
instead of hurting them.

One woman sat on the sidelines nursing a broken leg.
From a short distance, she looked like a man—tall and
slim, wearing Wrangler jeans and a baseball hat pulled
down tightly over closely cropped hair. She watched the
class every week with arms folded, cold eyes, and a sar-
castic smirk.

Something made me reach out to her. During the
prayer period, I always included her, asking God to heal
her so that she could dance with us. Sometimes she
would try to do some of the exercises from her seat.

The other instructors were afraid of her.

"Why do you talk to her? I just wish she would go
away; she's so mean-looking. We can't reach everyone,
you know, and she looks like a troublemaker."

"You know, that's the truth," offered one of the inmates.
"She's in here for life—murder. What a temper! She hit
another woman over the head with a baseball bat!"

But I knew I was no better than this inmate, who had
lost control and taken someone's life. My anger had been
equally as strong; there but for the grace of God most cer-
tainly went I. But having experienced this most destructive and debilitating emotion and found a healthy outlet,
I wanted to share it with these women.

This particular inmate slowly came around, and that
sinister smirk turned to a half-smile one night when she
turned to me and said, "You know, I like your program. I
could get into this. And I even like you—a little."

Other debilitating emotions stalk many inmates. One
is depression—frozen rage. Its dark slime is deeply
embedded in the walls of this women's penitentiary. Like
a serpent of despair, it slithers through cells, suffocating
its victims, manifesting itself in the blank stare, the
"prison shuffle."

Depression was an abstract ailment for me until I suffered my own after the rape. Like most people who are unacquainted with the malady firsthand, I hadn't an inkling of the true contours of depression or the nature of its pain.

Depression starts with a leaden and poisonous mood and develops into a deep melancholy—almost a mourning. Its victim becomes incapacitated. There is an emotional and physical distancing. Inactivity—an abrupt halt to normal activity—is the hallmark of depression.

She stood out in our dance class because of her talent, enthusiasm, and angelic good looks. Long, curly brown hair hung all the way down her back in artless, childish ripples and bounced merrily as she bopped to all the aerobic numbers. Pretty and petite, she would clasp her tiny hands with glee when I played her favorite song.

One time after class she told me, "This isn't only the best thing that has happened to me in prison; this is the best thing that has happened to me in my life."

She was one of our regulars. Faithfully she wrote out her prayer intentions each week and gave them to me. And the night when a new group of women—very tough, very insulting—came to class, she was our staunchest defender. She entreated the guards to forbid their attendance again. And she begged us, "Please come back next week. Don't let tonight upset you."

Then—for no reason—she stopped coming to class. I asked her friends, "Where is Tamara tonight?"

They looked from one to the other and then to the floor, all the while fidgeting and shuffling their feet.

"She's sick."

"She's sleeping."

And finally, "she's depressed."

Each week I would lift her up in prayer. I insisted that her friends tell her that I was asking for her and that I missed her. The third week, when they confessed about her depression, my words were measured but my message clear.

"Tell Tamara I understand. I, too, have been depressed. But I have a remedy, and maybe it will work for her too. First, turn it over to God because he cares. Next, keep busy and keep moving. It's the funniest thing; those are our two activities in this class—praying and moving to the music. Please tell her that I care about her and that there is a hole in my front row. Tell her to please come back."

Next week, in her usual spot, was my little friend. I hugged her and she took my hand, and with luminous brown eyes misty with emotion she said: "I came back because you cared. No one ever cared before."

Sometimes that's all it takes to dispel the cloud of depression.

But it is not that easy for most prisoners. The average inmate sees herself as a "loser," and feels it is "me against them." "Them" includes the police, courts, judges, lawyers, wardens, prison officers, chaplains, preachers, pastors, and churches. In most cases there has been very little commitment to God or a church. If she did have religious training in childhood, she now feels that God has let her down. She doubts her own security as a believer and is not at all sure that God will hear or answer her prayers. Typically, she feels that no one can love her—not even God.

Proudly she waved the two photos in front of me— before and after. The summer before starting my aerobics class, she weighed in at a hefty 275. Cocooned for years in a severely obese, dysfunctional body, now she was feeling good about herself, and ready to shed the failures of the past as well.

Perhaps this rebirth put her in a confessionary mood. But I wasn't prepared for what she divulged. Guiltless and with complete candor, she announced, "I'm in here for child molesting."

Seeing my look of shock she added, "Oh, it's not as bad as it sounds. It was just with some neighborhood kids, and they exaggerated."

They warn you before you go into prison not to ask the inmates what they are in for. But most of the time an inmate volunteers this information when you least expect it. I had just completed an hour's aerobics class. I was perspiring profusely and frantically gathering my tapes before the guards locked the gym for the night when she decided to tell all.

The only response I could muster was "I'll pray for you."

I did pray for her that night, and I asked God to give me wisdom in this situation. I could understand anger and depression on some level, but perversion with little children was something I couldn't stomach.

Why she made me privy to this appalling information I will never know. I was an aerobics instructor. I could encourage her about weight loss. But child molesting was out of my realm.

In retrospect, piecing together bits of information, I realized that she was desperately trying to be accepted for herself. She needed constant affirmation in class.

"I practiced the dance steps in my cell this week. Did you notice?"

I also found out later that she had been abused as a child—a fact quite common among inmates, both male and female. It's a circular dance of perversion, abuse, molestation that continues on from generation to generation. A child who is abused becomes an adult who abuses . . . and on and on.

Besides praying and pointing her to the "Great Physician" who can make her whole, the best that I could do for this inmate was to encourage her in her newfound self-esteem, never judge her, and always love her.

I learned a lot about nonjudgmental love from a beautiful woman, the wife of a minister, who has had a prison ministry for seven years. She sums up the responsibility of a prison volunteer: "They come to us half-dead, abused, broken, angry, bitter. Our job is to love them back to life."

And love them she does! Through her actions I have seen the amazing power of love.

Before our dance ministry was to begin, we went to a prison volleyball game to do some public relations for our aerobics program. It was the prisoners versus the church volunteers, including this woman.

When the game was over, the guard came in to round up the inmates.

"Wait, I have to say a quick prayer," this woman begged.

"I just want you to know that the reason we come in here is because Jesus loves you, and we love you. . . ."

I had been watching the meanest-looking prisoner, a cap covering all semblance of a feminine haircut. Suddenly she softened: "And we love you too." Her voice trembled, and a tear stained her cheek.

The power of love.

I also learned sensitivity from this woman. When I was preparing my dance numbers, I would say: "I have these great songs for my prisoners."

She would temper my enthusiasm with a caution: "Honey, they're our ladies, not our prisoners. They're human beings, and if we treat them kindly and with dignity and the love of Jesus, we'll reach them."

When I first talked to my pastor about my dance ministry, he told me that he thought that my testimony would be effective with these women. He said, "When I go into the prison, they scoff at me and say I don't know what it is like to be abused. And I have to agree with them. But you do. Tell them your story. It will make an impression. You might be their wounded healer."

I haven't shared my testimony before a large group in prison, but I have individually. Once I had this response: "God must really love us a lot to send you in here. It's people like some of our brothers and fathers and boyfriends that rape and rob. Is that why you always talk about how Jesus forgives in our prayer time?"

It is true that I always emphasized forgiveness. Jesus forgave me for my sins. I forgave the rapist. And that is the continuing pattern of Christianity. It is amazing to witness the healing power of forgiveness among the inmates. If they know that they are forgiven and accepted, a burden seems to lift from their shoulders, and they express hope for the future.

Besides forgiveness, I centered my prayers around different themes every week: salvation, living above our circumstances, healing for both souls and bodies, and power over weaknesses.

When I spoke about frailties I included bad companions and addictions to food, alcohol, or drugs. I prayed that God would give us all power over our failings and help us conquer our addictions.

Ninety-nine percent of the offenses committed by female inmates are drug related. Crimes such as passing bad checks, shoplifting, robbery, and prostitution are often committed to purchase drugs. Many of the women are also addicts, and they are recovering through treatment programs within the prison. I was told by the chaplain that many of the prison's behavior problems had joined our aerobics class and that she had seen them change. She encouraged their participation.

I often remind them when we are in prayer that the body is the temple of the spirit and that we must respect it, cherish it, and thank God for it. I encourage them in aerobics to hone their bodies to the nth degree—to discipline them, control them, master their weaknesses, to love them.

Her family had dubbed her the "golden girl" because she won a "beautiful baby" contest as an infant. She had dreams of becoming a model. But for an abandoned wife at age eighteen with two children, such a career was out of the question. Faced with the grim reality of raising her family alone, she turned to heroin to mask her fear and her pain. In a private nightmare of drugs, depression, and disastrous liaisons, her life spiraled ever downward. The once flawless model's body now was covered with needle marks and bruises. She recalls vividly the night she was arrested and what followed:

"I was cold—colder than I have ever been in my life. But I kept walking. I had to have it. The neighborhood was real seedy, and I shuddered when I thought of my two kids at home. I had left them in front of Sesame Street and a bowl of Spaghettios. I hoped I would be back before the program was over.

"I saw him in the distance, pacing nervously, looking from side to side.

"'What took you so long?' he snapped.

"I reached into my jacket for the wad of bills I had removed from the cookie jar—this month's rent.

"'Did you tell anyone about this meeting place? . . . 'cuz. . . .'

"They seemed to come out of nowhere. Blue lights flashing. Three cruisers. I was caught. A felon. My life would never be the same. I had hit rock bottom—the dark side of the dream. My end.

"Sometime during the horrors of withdrawal, I decided to turn my life around. I was gonna get it right this time. Learn something while I'm in here. Go to school. Get a trade. I also wanted to get healthy. That's why I came to aerobics. Then I started thinking about some of the prayers that you say at the end of class. And I decided that I needed to get it right with God. One night I asked Jesus to come into my life. I asked him to help me change. I began to read the Bible, and I'm really trying to do what it says. I have a job in here. I work with other inmates, and sometimes they complain about the work. I remember what the Bible says about going the extra mile, and I ask if I can help them.

"You know, I'm gonna make it this time, because I'm okay in here."

She smiled, pointing to her heart.

And then there was the phenomenon of the T-shirts!

Both guards and inmates were intrigued by Psalm 30:11 on our backs. The chaplain told us that many had requested Bibles to look up the text on the back of our shirts. It became our group insignia. All the girls wanted one.

One explained, "I look at you and I think to myself, I could be like her. She dances, and she's funny. The only difference between us is that you seem to love this Jesus, and he makes you happy. Now I have a T-shirt and a Bible. Maybe I can know him, too, and be like you."

10

Wounded Healer
in a Dance Symphony

She had style and presence—eyes sparkling, lips red, a body transformed by a few simple arm and torso moves. At nineteen, still an urchin underneath, she handled herself with the discipline and confidence of a bareback rider in the circus, making the most difficult trick look easy. She was electric. She dazzled. She was a showstopper. You can always spot one.

"You really move well," I gushed.

"I never thought that I would be in an aerobic dance class. But I do have experience—sort of. I was a stripper in a downtown nightclub. They pulled me in for that and prostitution."

"Well, if you wanted to become a legitimate, professional dancer or choreographer, I could help you. I really believe if you set your mind to it, you could make it."

"That's my dream." Her voice trembled with emotion.

"Let's start with having you choreograph a song for the class. This is how you write it out. You can finish it this week and show me your creation next week. I can bring you a reading list of all the great choreographers. And I can recommend many dance teachers and schools when you get out."

I learned that before you can make any progress with inmates, you have to be able to look them in the eye and say, "I believe in you." And mean it.

I noticed a change when the girls saw that we believed in them. Some of them tried so hard to please us: practicing during the week, thanking us profusely, and beaming when they heard a compliment on their dancing:

"Good job! Great technique! Looking good!"

If I owned my own health club or dance studio, I would have said to many of them: "When you get out, I'd like to train you to be an instructor in my club."

I truly believe that if they knew that someone believed in them, and if they were doing something that they liked, they would handle the responsibility and stay straight.

I gave the women a prayer that we said every week. I found it in a book; untitled and anonymous. I dubbed it the Dancer's Prayer:

> Giver of life, Creator of all that is lovely,
>   Teach me to sing the words to your song;
> I want to feel the music of living
>   And not fear the sad songs,
> But from them make new songs
>   Composed of both laughter and tears.
>
> Teach me to dance to the sounds of your world
>   and your people,
>   I want to move in rhythm with your plan;
> Help me to try to follow your leading,

> To risk even falling,
> To rise and keep trying
> Because you are leading the dance.

After a couple of months, the women brought in prayer requests every week. They had concerns about their families, about prison life, and about their future. Every week the prayer time got longer and aerobics a little shorter. As their belief grew, so did the requests, and they started to verbalize their prayers with me.

The average prison inmate today is under twenty-five years of age and comes from a broken home or from a home where there was little love or discipline. She has had nine years of schooling but actually acquired only a seventh-grade education. She has very little vocational training and has usually worked for a minimum wage, if she has worked at all.

These are just some of the reasons why an inmate has such poor self-esteem and is terrified of trying to exist in a society that brands her a loser, a troublemaker, an outcast. But with the help of the Lord, someone to believe in her, and a chance, she really can change.

I didn't always believe this. For a long while after the rape, I strongly advocated the death penalty. I thought that heinous crimes such as rape should be punishable by death. In fact, during my anger phase I used to make the statement that I would actually pull the lever on the electric chair to rid society of these sadistic criminals.

Well-meaning friends would back me up and say that the Old Testament talked about the wrath of God against evildoers and that God was only against murder without just cause. But I had a Sunday school teacher who pointed to that same Old Testament, cited Noah and the flood, and reminded us that God said he would never destroy humanity in this way again. This teacher interpreted this as a plea against taking a life for any reason.

My change of mind is based not only on such biblical evidence, but my experience with the prisoners.

When we came into prison as the Joy Dancers, we gave them a rope to grab onto—a chance for salvation, a chance for fun and fellowship, and—with the music and the movement—the chance to dance. I saw the cynical faces that entered class every week and the faces that left. There was joy on those faces.

I once read a fairy tale about twin brothers. As they got older, one of the boys left home and involved himself in debauchery and evil living. He met a magician who turned him into a wolf because of his sins.

Years later, the other brother was walking through the woods and was attacked by his brother, the wolf. Rather than defend himself, the brother simply looked with compassion and great love at the ferocious wolf. And as he did, the wolf features became human again and the brother was restored.

The power of love can change anyone.

After the rape I had only two choices—hate or love. I could either hate the men who assaulted me and others like them, both male and female, or I could learn to love them.

I chose love.

I have been on both sides—from the cruel stories of man's inhumanity to man resonating through the line-ups to the softening of a hardened convict who has met the Lord.

My commitment is to bring these two worlds together, because I have a unique experience in both.

In my own small way I see myself bridging the gap. And because I have known the nightmare, I can foster the dream.

Everything that I believe and everything that I have become is because of the rape. My life cannot be separated from it.

I have heard individuals speak about their adversity and say, "Despite the pain and suffering, I would never trade this experience for anything."

Would I?

I have to be honest, as I have tried to be throughout this book. I shudder to think of going through the rape experience again. It hurt. Recovery took many years, and I still have the battle scars to prove it.

And yet, I cannot say I would want to go back to being the person I was.

I was showing an older and wiser friend of mine two photos: one of me before the rape and one after. He made an interesting observation: "The picture of you before the rape is quite lovely. Your skin is smooth. No wrinkles. You are unsmiling but determined. The eyes are direct and focused. Unflinching. Cold.

"The other picture has many battle scars. It shows the toll that suffering has taken. But the smile is warm. And look at those eyes! There is love in those eyes."

Pain and suffering bring us to a fork in the road. It is not possible to remain unchanged. You can let the anger and bitterness eat away at you, or you can let it transform you.

It has been said that adversity introduces a person to her true self. I like the new woman I met. Underneath the superficial façade of the shallow dancer I used to be was someone genuine, someone caring, someone strong.

When I first began the prison ministry, I wanted to be an example. I wanted to tell the inmates about the Lord, to encourage them about physical fitness, but I also wanted to keep my distance. But something happened as the weeks wore on. I really started to care about each woman as an individual—precious in God's sight, with the potential to do great things.

After I was raped, I couldn't have children.

Never will I know my own baby's cry, the feel of my fuzzy-haired infant cradled in my arms, a chorus of contagious coos and squeals, that special intimacy known only to mother and child. For years I shed bitter tears, wondering how God could allow this additional suffering.

Then one night in prayer it came to me.

They are your children. They want to please you. They need someone to believe in them. And you have a mother's love. Give it to them.

Maybe that is why I care so much.

The recidivism rate is very high among inmates. They return to the same neighborhoods, the same friends, and often the same habits.

I'm not claiming that my ministry is a total panacea; I'm not a pollyanna. But after these inmates have been Joy Dancers, they go back to their neighborhoods having heard the gospel every week, armed with T-shirts bearing the word of God, and with a blueprint for a healthy lifestyle. And if I, empowered by Jesus Christ and working as his instrument, can prevent it by words, deeds, and fervent prayers, they will at least think twice before they commit another crime.

I have never felt the presence of God as strongly as I have in prison during the worship services and among the women believers. His presence is almost palpable; he makes himself available to suffering people. Much has been cynically written about jailhouse conversions, but I have seen those sincere and repentant souls, and they are earnest in their decision.

I also believe that the Lord blesses those who reach out to hurting people. I feel his presence in my dance class every week. I hear the Master's voice whispering my cues, holding me up when I'm bone tired, and smiling down on a dance group founded for his purposes.

To paraphrase a line from the movie *Chariots of Fire:* "When I dance, I can feel his pleasure." And then I pass on that pleasure and try to break through the cycle of misery with the joy the Lord has given me.

I guess this joy is evident not only in my feet but on my face as well. Friends have said that I glow when I speak about the dance ministry, and people pick this up, especially the inmates.

This Christmas we had a recital where the prisoners performed all their dance numbers in red Joy Dancers T-shirts, their gifts to keep. The audience was comprised of other prisoners and members of my church. One woman remarked, "Your face is luminous when you are dancing. It is like you are in a circle of light—a divine spotlight—and it radiates to all around you."

I truly believe it is the joy of the Lord.

The Bible says that God uses the foolish of the world to confound the wise. And every week I see him use something as foolish as dance to confound. It confounds the prison guards when six women in pink T-shirts can control murderers, thieves, and addicts. It confounds and silences the skeptics who question such a dance program. And it confounds them all when at the end of every class sixty sweaty, tired women gather in a circle and join hands to pray—and at the name of Jesus every head bows. It confounds them all except, of course, the great Choreographer, who is there among us.

I have a dream, and I have shared this dream with the inmates. The dream is that when I die and meet the Lord, he will say to me, "There are some people here waiting to see you. It is real easy to pick them out because they all arrived here in costume."

And from every side they will come, in shirts as color-ful as their lives were on earth. And those whom the world called trash, he will call trophies. Quickly we will assemble in a chorus line. I'll take my place among them—their wounded healer. And we will perform for the Lord a dance symphony.

His eyes will dance as we dance, and he will smile on a ministry founded in his name. And as we finish, very slowly but very deliberately, he will lift two nail-scarred hands, and he will applaud.

N otes

EPIGRAM

Calvin Miller, *The Singer* (Downers Grove, Ill.: InterVarsity Press, 1975), 145.

CHAPTER 4 *The Dancer Returns*

1. Corrie ten Boom *Each New Day* (Old Tappan, N.J.: Revell, 1977), 109–10.

CHAPTER 6 *Forgiveness: His Signature Piece*

1. Charles Swindoll, *Improving Your Serve* (Waco, Tex.: Word, 1981).

CHAPTER 7 *New Steps for a New Life*

1. *The Dance Notebook* (Philadelphia: Running Press, 1984).
2. Based on a speech given by Tom Sullivan at the "Celebrate 1983" Million Dollar Roundtable, Dallas, Texas.
3. Corrie ten Boom, *The Hiding Place* (Old Tappan, N.J.: Revell, 1961), 161.

CHAPTER 8 *Enter the Joy Dancers*

1. Adapted from "When You Pray" by Audrey May Mieir.